MW00453281

We Write the Letters That Heal

Compiled by
Carolyn Coleman

We Write the Letters That Heal

Compiled by
Carolyn Coleman

The Lady of Wisdom Publishing Company

The Lady of Wisdom Publishing Company
4542 Robinson Rd.
Jackson, Mississippi 39284

Published by The Lady of Wisdom Publishing Company June 30, 2023.

ISBN: 978-1-7342352-3-4 (paperback)
ISBN: 978-1-7342352-4-1 (eBook)

Library of Congress Control Number: 2023910929

Table of Contents

Introduction

"To appoint unto them that mourn in Zion, to give unto them beauty for ashes, the oil of joy for mourning, the garment of praise for the spirit of heaviness; that they might be called trees of righteousness, the planting of the LORD, *that he might be glorified"* (Isaiah 61:3).

The word broken originates from "break" which means shabar in Hebrew. The Webster dictionary defines broken as:

- Shattered
- Damaged or altered by or as if by breaking
- Not working properly
- Being irregular, interrupted, or full of obstacles
- Violated by transgression not kept or honored

Each of us has faced brokenness at some instance in our lives. It can be emotional, financial, physical, spiritual, etc. The aftermath of these challenges can make us feel as if we have been dealt a bad hand or that we have been forgotten about. In Isaiah 61:3, the Scripture notes that you would receive "beauty for ashes." Ashes can be a reference to a place of lowliness or grief. In Job 30:19, it

states, *"He hath cast me into the mire, and I am become like dust and ashes."* How else could we witness God's grace and mercy without the actual experience?

One may ask, how does healing take place? What procedural methods cause healing to happen? This book is written with the intent to give insight, healing, revelation, and effective communication to the reader. The selected authors divinely handcrafted each letter to express experiences from their personal lives. In this anthology, readers will learn how to grow from the traumas that may plague their current existence. The letters are transparently written and done so they will understand that each author is quite different but shares commonalities which create a theme for this compilation. In each life lesson, the especially important notions of healing are emphasized. The healing concepts are not repetitive from one author to the other, instead, they are made more precise.

We Write the Letters That Heal provides a comprehensive explanation of physical healing, spiritual healing, and mental healing. It gives vivid affirmations to heal, overcome, and thrive in life. Readers will be informed, encouraged, and enlightened to continue their quest for healing. The author's presentation is logical, practical, and grounded in transparent common intellectual terms. This book will help the reader understand the complexities of their life and how God gives them beauty for the ashes. No one has to stay in a mindset of being abandoned, unloved, misunderstood, or

abused. There is hope for everyone to overcome.

This book will aide you in picking up the broken pieces and becoming the best version of yourself. We hope that our stories are a guiding light as you begin your pathway to wholeness. It is your season to rise up and declare, "I am more than enough. It is my time and I will not miss it looking back. I am ready for the exchange of ashes to beauty and sorrow to joy."

Letters Written By
Dr. Carolyn Coleman

To My Daughter Nichole, I Thank God for the Masterpiece of You

To My Daughter Nichole:

You have sacrificed to see my dreams come true. Now, I sacrifice to see your dreams and aspirations become your reality. I am so grateful for the woman, mother, community servant leader, and entrepreneur you have become.

I have been an eyewitness to your struggles and victories. What I admire is your faith to stay in the race. Your beauty and quick wit have made you a target of those who settled and dared not to strive for more.

You have suffered unfair treatment in the workplace among foes clothed as friends, but you did not become bitter. In life, you must dress for every occasion and be willing to ride out every storm. The eagle in you knows how to fly above the storm and defeat the enemy with prayer and praise. You are the epitome of God's will. He gave you beauty for ashes and joy for all your sorrows.

Your faith and determination to not quit is your superpower wrapped in love. God has navigated you through your red sea and favor and prosperity are your portion. Choose to always see the light in the darkness. Proclaim your cup is always running over with abundance even when you can't see it. Remember the good and cast the bad things up to God quickly. Always remember the power of **next**. Never get stuck on stupid. Every battle is not yours to fight. Always, consult God for direction. He will order your steps and direct your path.

Continue to live a life of honor before your daughter. She will watch and mimic what you do more than what you say. You may think she is not listening to what you are teaching her, but she is. Children do listen even when they pretend not to. Pray for God to guide her and keep her safe from harm. Pray nightly that she has an increase in discernment, wisdom, knowledge, and understanding. Pray for an inner circle of God-fearing friends. Speak and declare the Deuteronomy 11:1 blessing over both of your lives. Pray for multiple increases in her ability to put pen to paper and prosper. Yes, pray without ceasing and ask God to put a hedge of protection around her.

You are now navigating new waters in your life. Put the pains and disappointments of the past in your rearview mirror. Do not take the burdens of divorce and place them at the feet of a new relationship. That would cheat you and steal the joy of a new chapter. Your 'next' should not have to pay for the mistakes and missteps of a previous relationship. Let the muddy water of the past

go, so you can live, love, prosper, and stay in peace. Yes, you deserve love. I pray for the hand of God to guide you and show you the man who will love, respect, value, and honor you and your daughter.

While looking after the baby, don't forget the importance of self-love. Show yourself grace and keep moving forward. I believe in you. Greatness is attached to your name. Claim and name your happiness. Believe in yourself and see yourself as God sees you a masterpiece deserving of all things good.

Speak these words over yourself in times of trouble: "I give myself permission to cry. God will read my tears and identify my moans and groans. He will download the directives necessary to dismantle and destroy the plots of the wicked. Now is my time to dig in, fight and win. I fight on my knees knowing that the battle is not mine, it is the Lord's. God will rescue me and destroy the wicked. Greater is He that is living within me than any outside forces. My DNA has equipped me for battle and assured me of ultimate victory. I will not allow envy, jealousy, malice, and the insecurities of others to rob me of my joy, peace, love, health, prosperity, and happiness. I am wise enough and strong enough to step over offenses. I proudly put on my eagle wings and soar above the storms. I can do all things through Jesus Christ who strengthens me. No weapon formed against me shall prosper."

Love Always,
Mama

<u>Affirmation</u>

I am excited about the new thing God is doing in my life. I will not waste time looking back when life is calling me to move forward. I am worthy of the good things in life. I trust I Am to guide me well as I navigate the waters of a new beginning.

The Precious Gift of a Granddaughter

Dear Granddaughter,

You have brought bright sunshine, awesome blue skies, and a melody of love and laughter to my life. I rejoiced from the moment I heard about your coming.

I had longed to be a grandmother. My grandmothers died before I could experience their love, touch, and wisdom. I starved for their hugs and words of wisdom as a child.

My first grandchild did not live to see the dawning of the day. Then God blessed us with you. At age three, out of the blue, you said, "Nana, I knew you before I was born." I smiled and said, "I knew you too."

I prayed to God to keep you safe in your mother's womb. One night, I asked God if He would take another grandchild from me. That night, I drifted into a deep sleep, yet I was wide awake. I saw God lift you from your mother's womb and speak life to you. He eased my fears and assured me you would be born healthy. I shouted over the victory.

We have spent many Saturday mornings talking and laughing over bacon, grits, and eggs. I always sprinkled words of wisdom in between each bite.

It's important to think for yourself. Treat yourself with love and respect. Applaud others and applaud yourself. Honor and love God. Reverence your parents and listen attentively to their instructions. Read and write every day, it will bring joy and healing to you. Do your very best and never laugh at others. Find solace in laughing at yourself. You frame your world with the words you speak, the actions you take, and the thoughts that rehearse in your mind. Call on God daily and know that He is your friend. Life may change and friends may come and go but stay true to yourself and extend grace to yourself and others.

You are God's masterpiece, fearfully and wonderfully made, designed and crafted for greatness. Never surrender to doubt and fear. Remember Yet and Next. Be willing to stretch and never quit in life. Be you on purpose and go and conquer the world.

Love Always,
Nana

Affirmation

I am called by God to heal nations, speak truth, and walk in the light of Jesus Christ. I am more than enough. I am empowered to bud, blossom and bloom at the same time. I am living the abundant life in Christ. He has made me bold and courageous. I am fearfully and wonderfully made in Jesus' Name. I live and flow in the great riches of God. I am a recipient of Father Abraham with more than enough blessings in health, wealth, power, riches, faith, and love. I live and flow in the great riches of God. My faith is unstoppable and the rewards of it have caused the enemy to flee and prosperity to flow from the north, south, east, and west. I am unstoppable with God.

Letter to God for the New Year

Dear God,

I thank You for bringing me through the ups and downs, and the lows and highs of last year. I thank You for not allowing my enemy to triumph over me. Through all the processing and growth of the past year, I have come to know, value, and appreciate You. My trials, tribulations, and yes, even my pains have brought me closer to You. I applaud You for being my company, keeper, comforter, and yes, my peace. You kept my mind and gave me strength beyond my comprehension. You provided resources that I could not see and extended grace in my moment of weakness and uncertainty.

I wake to the dawn of a new year and new opportunities recognizing that I do not have time to waste looking back and rehearsing the past. It is the **Next** that you have instilled in me that has transformed my sense of urgency to live free from regret. You have shown me the blueprint for a happy life, and I thank You. Forgetting those things that are behind me, my daily assignment is to keep pressing forward with a grateful heart. I joyfully make You the head of my household and the person I seek out to order my steps and thoughts daily. *You are the center of my soul and priority number one.*

I am being ushered into the possibility of a fresh start. New opportunities, friends, challenges, and changes are popping into my head. I find myself excited to do and be more and to challenge myself to believe in the greater. The opportunity to do more for You and others is exploding in my Spirit.

Unlike years before, I will not take for granted the gift of breath. I treasure each breath and applaud You for the gift of life. No more rushing into my day and forgetting who made this day. No more making You an afterthought and calling on You only in an emergency. You will be the first person I greet each morning and the last person I talk with at night. When I wake, my lips will sing of Your glorious goodness and Your tender mercies that surround me day by day.

I will journal my thoughts and prayers daily reflecting on what I am grateful for. I stand in agreement and proclaim Lamentations 3:22-23 (ESV), *"The steadfast love of the LORD never ceases; his mercies never come to an end; they are new every morning; great is your faithfulness."* I will not faint at what is to come. I know You have already charted my day. I will speak victory in the face of defeat. I will choose to be happy in times of despair. I will shout the victory over every battle that I face. I know that You are with me, fighting for me and grooming and arming me with the tools needed to overcome any sickness or disease. I am battled tested and battle ready to handle any foe, situation, or trick of the enemy. I am no longer afraid of the unknown because I know You are living within me. My faith is attached to Your faithfulness and therefore I cannot fail.

You have charted my days and filled them with favor

and grace attached to mercy and forgiveness in every scenario of my life. I am implementing a trio communication plan of action. I will encourage three people per day. In a week, I will have intentionally encouraged twenty-one people. In a month, eighty-four people.

I am thirsty to be Your voice on the earth. I desire to honor every person You have assigned to my life. No longer will I pray in silence when people are starving to hear that someone cares and is praying on their behalf. I can do nothing without You, Father God, but I can do all things through You. I love You and freely put all my trust in You. I am determined and charged to be a weapon of power in the hands of a Mighty God. Usher me into the depth of Your presence and endow me with Your Spirit and love.

In Jesus' Name, Amen.

Affirmation

I am wrapped in the magnificence of God's beauty and Holiness. Formed in the righteousness of my Savior and elevated in mind, body and soul. I am a force of nature. Weaponized to defeat demons, devils, and foes. Created for a divine purpose and armored by my faith. Wrapped in God's amazing grace that leads and guides me to unimaginable victories in the most unexpected places. Glorious, gracious, loving God, it is You who carved the heavens and sculptured the earth. Thank You for giving me the gift of life.

Words of Wisdom to
My Daughters in the Gospel

Dear Daughters in the Gospel,

Do not put your trust in fame, fortune, people, or your knowledge. This walk will require you to surrender to and trust in God. Never chase down lies. A lie will not last forever and will be proven false in the end.

Do not believe those who say they will always be with you. More often than expected, they will not. Never doubt that God is for you. He is working behind the scenes when He seems the farthest from you. Do not get caught up in the politics of ministry.

Never be the Judas to your fellow cohorts in the gospel. Do not put money before the needs of your congregation.

Never make your family secondary to the Church. Your family deserves your time and attention too. Do not be afraid to ask for help and be willing to receive sound advice.

Never allow the pain and disappointments of missteps to keep you down. The ability to get up quickly, determined to not rehash or replay the same error in judgment, is your right of passage.

Do not preach a sermon based on bias to send a private message of dissent. Your pulpit is to teach, instruct and guide. It is not to be used as a bully pulpit

against a foe, family, or member of the congregation.

Never believe that you can do this walk alone. You will need a village, mentors, and a confidant in ministry.

Do not neglect the importance of having a protective, wise, disciplined inner circle sold out to God. Jesus had twelve disciples and one was a thief. He had three in His inner circle, Peter, James, and John, that He asked to pray for Him in His most trying moments on earth. Always, respect and honor the power of three and know your go-to three.

Never ask others to do or give more than you are willing to do and give. Do not mishandle the love that others have for you.

Never neglect your need to love yourself. Self-care is necessary to maintain good health, happiness, and peace of mind.

Love,
Mama CC

Affirmation

I am never going to allow the opinions of others to dictate my level of success and belief in myself. I am determined to be happy, healthy, wealthy, prosperous, and filled with joy unspeakable. I am who God says I am.

Never Be Defined By the Labels of Others

Dear Reader,

Do not allow the size of your lips, hips, or fingertips to make you doubt or mistrust your ability to succeed. Don't quit a job before you complete the application because you feel like you are not good enough.

Never allow the labels of a few to define who you are or who you can become. The neighborhood you grew up in does not determine your next address.

Take every negative in your life and make it a positive.

Do not get caught in the comparison game. You are not in competition with anyone but yourself. If you have the skills, do not allow doubt to destroy your will to go after what you want in life.

Don't allow the enemy to steal your promise before you step into it.

Refuse the voices that come to break your spirit with lies like you don't have the right clothes, automobile, education, or live in the right neighborhood to be successful.

When you wear designer clothes, no one knows if they came from Dirt Cheap, Goodwill, or Macy's. Pray and ask God to teach you when to speak and when to be silent.

I thank God for Mama who taught me to love me. She told us to reach for the moon and we might catch a falling star. On your worst day, get up, put on your best

suit and sweetest-smelling perfume, best makeup, and act like you have a million even if you don't have a dime to your name. She taught me how to envision an outcome greater than my condition. I learned how to visualize, frame, and redirect my thoughts which brings elevation and manifestations. It is faith in action motivated by visualization and expectation. Yes, you can call those things that are not and see them happen. This is your moment to conquer your fears. Speak the truth to yourself. See yourself as God sees you and walk or dance your way into your new life. You are beautiful, talented, and creative so live, love, forgive, be healed, and prosper indeed as your soul prospers.

Yours truly,
Dr. Carolyn Coleman

Affirmation

I am faithful and truly committed to living for God. Opportunities, partnerships, business, and financial blessings now daily chase my bank account, checkbook, pocketbook, and all places where my money is stored. I am not willing to be labeled by man when God is my source.

Everlasting Love

Dear Carolyn,

Everlasting love cannot be broken, borrowed, or stolen. It edifies the soul. It strengthens and embraces everyone that it meets. Every pit of fire has taken you higher. Love shelters, protects, and assures you that he will never leave you. In the belly of the whale, you discovered you are a diamond and a pearl. The testing was building a legacy of unconditional love. You learned how to love the unlovable and forgive the unforgivable because of the valleys and mountains you had to navigate through to accomplish your dreams and goals.

You are laughing at life and taking everything in stride. Teaching others how to step over and move on with pride. You have conquered the unknown and resurrected so many lost souls. The intentionality and fierceness of your love completely shut down hate. It is God who gets the glory, make no mistake. He created love and love is living and operating in you. Kudos to you.

Love,
Carolyn

<u>Affirmation</u>

I am love molded and created in the image of God. I freely spread love and it freely returns to me.

The Real Black Man

Dear Black Man,

You are the pride and joy of your mother. You are the weapon that builds up strong roots that time and circumstances cannot shake loose or divide. You are the shoulders that daughters lean on. You are the strength that builds your woman up and never lets her down. I see your beauty and your strength and salute you for all the wrong things that you have endured. Let me stop and applaud you for all you went through. Thank you, my brother and King. Stand tall and know that you are not alone. I am so proud of you and pray for you continuously.

Yours truly,
A Proud Black Woman,

<u>Affirmation</u>

I am your friend. Make me proud of you. Do not accept labels and do not become a label. Be you with joy, respect, honor, and truth and you can always count on me.

Money is My Friend

"A feast is made for laughter, and wine maketh
merry; but money answereth all things"
(Ecclesiastes 10:19. KJV).

Dear Reader,

I am money. Money is me. I have found the key to her longevity. Invite her into your life and command her to multiply and increase daily in your pocketbook and bank accounts. If you command her with love to stay, she will visit you every day. Money wants to be your friend. Send her an invitation and welcome her into your life.

I have learned to respect her and never neglect her. I give her commands and she obeys. Money comes to me from the north, south, east, and west. I never dismiss her nor dishonor her worth and value. So, in my pocketbook, bank accounts and more she loves to rest. I give her instructions on what to pay. Quickly, she goes and returns with a greater flow of capital and dividends than ever before.

I give instructions and I know certain words I can never say to or about her. Money is sentimental and wants to be needed. Never use the word SPEND. Never talk badly or say you do not need her. She is sensitive, you see.

If you respect her, she will serve you with joy all the days of your life without strife. Her assignment is to meet your monetary needs.

Sincerely,
The Lady of Wisdom

<u>Affirmation</u>

I am money and money is me. I respect her and she will obey me. I call on the energy of money and welcome her in to my pocketbooks, bank accounts and more.

You Shall Live On In Me

Dear Daddy,

Death called for you and you had to answer. One day, I will have to answer too. Know that as long as there is air in my lungs, you will live on in me. Your beautiful smile and quiet charm kept me safe from harm. I always felt protected and loved by you.

Daddy, as I travel back down memory lane, the Christmas stories of Santa Claus and jingle bell fighting and all the hysteria of the holidays still fill my heart with joy. I rejoice reflecting on past Christmas celebrations. I smell the smoke that filled the air from firecrackers, smoke bombs, sparklers, and so much more. I still hear Mama saying, "John Henry, you ought to be ashamed of yourself telling those stories." You were the storyteller in the family. I believed every one. You taught me how to laugh, have fun and be comfortable in my skin.

Your memories have not faded with time. Your love has not diminished because you transitioned to the other side. No, you gave me a lifetime of memories like our first and last fishing trip. While teaching me how to drive you said hit the gas pedal and go. I even remember your favorite and only TV show you watched faithfully every Monday night at 6:30 (Gun Smoke). Sometimes, I watch it just to feel close to you.

I will always treasure and never bury the precious moments and memories of you. You made me laugh and

21

believe that I was special. I thank God for your life, sacrifices, love, and care you provided for me. I love you, Daddy, rest in peace.

Your Baby Girl,
Sue

Affirmation

    I am so proud of the life you shared with me. You will live on because I will continue to share our memories. Rest in peace.

The Complexities of Love

Dear Reader,

How do I begin to tell you that love is not a sin? It was here from the beginning and will be here to the very end. Love is passion. Love is peace. Love is joy. Love is messy and sometimes hard to explain.

How can love be so perplexing? Is it not supposed to be a blessing? Yes, my daughter's love is a blessing. Like life, sometimes it can be bewildering and complicated. Yet, it is joyful and fulfilling, and stimulating to the heart.

Think of it like this: Love is the gathering of hearts and the mingling and blending of minds. Two hearts touch and love erupts. Two eyes meet and two hands dance in and out of place within the same beat.

Two legs intermingle and their bodies collide. Electricity, energy, magic and laughter, and heavenly motion in the ocean shows up and declares new life. It is explosive, delicate, and gentle, yet it sets the soul free.

Love always,
Dr. Carolyn Coleman

<u>Affirmation</u>

I am young. Not ready for love but needing to know and understand its delicacies. Share the truth of what it should be. So, when Mr. Right discovers me, I will marry him in white with a three-chord attachment that came from Heaven to me.

Forced Promotion

To Every Person Who Has Been Fired Wrongly from a Job:

You stood tall through all the lies and false attacks that were hurled at you. When wrongly fired, you could have retaliated. You could have been bitter and broken. Oh, no, you held your head up and declared it was a forced promotion from God.

You amazed me with how you stood on your faith and trusted God to see you through it all. I love the poems and songs, the books, and the sermons that were born as a result of your firing and false allegations of wrongful conduct. Truly, what the enemy planned for bad, God turned for your good.

Thank you for standing up for right even if it left you standing alone or so it appeared. In the end, you fought to clear your name. Even after being advised that you should sue them for lies, false allegations, and personal attacks, you stood firm. You wanted your name cleared and the truth revealed. God blessed you to prove your innocence. Vengeance belongs to God. You put them all in His hands.

Look at you now, established as a leader, preacher, teacher, author, and advocate for others. I salute you for your faith and courage. You never wavered in your faith in God to see you through. Look at you. You are speaking, teaching, writing, singing, and spreading God's

Word to the world. You always said the assignment of haters, foes, and critics was to elevate you and bring God's favor. It was forced promotion. When a man fires you, God will hire you. Oh, how sweet that is. Thank You, God, for forced promotions with unimaginable dividends.

Victory over the enemy,
Love Mama

Affirmation

You thought firing me was going to defeat me. You didn't understand it was God's plan for my next level of elevation. It was forced promotion. That which the enemy sent for bad, God has turned it for my good. I am forced promotion.

About the Author

Bishop Coleman is the Founder and Bishop of the Tabernacle of Alpha & Omega Non-Denominational Church in Jackson, Mississippi.

She received a Bachelor of Science in Mass Communications and a Master of Science in Library Science and Educational Technology from Jackson State University, and a PhD in Philosophy and Human Relations from The Dayspring Christian University. She is also a Certified Licensed Christian Master Life Coach, Author, and Public Speaker.

Dr. Coleman is the Founder and Executive Director of C Squared Educational Resource Center "An Accredited Academic Institution" in Jackson, Mississippi, and the Executive Director of the TA&O Mentoring Program.

She's the former Executive Director of Kids Kollege and the Children Defense Fund Freedom School at JSU. In 2017, Bishop Coleman was appointed Academic Dean of DCCJ Kingdom Theological Seminary. Among her many honors is the President's Higher Education Community Service Award for Excellence in Hurricane Relief Service.

Letters Written By
Trudy Barksdale

Moving Without Delay

Dear Reader,

It was the nine spiritual disciplines that caused elevation in my ministry. I constantly walked in procrastination while waiting until the last minute to complete a task or make sound decisions. I was overthinking everything and feeling depleted. In an act of desperation, I signed up for a class that changed the trajectory of my life. No more moving in delay, it was time to commit to walking and operating in faith.

It was the introduction to the nine spiritual disciplines that sparked and ignited true worship, ministry, and faith in God. Praying, worshiping, Bible studying, fasting, fellowshipping, confessing of my sins, examining my life, consecrating myself, and meditating on God awakened the true power of the Holy Spirit. Applying those disciplines has made an unforgettable impact on my life. I pray that this testimony will cause others to move without delay.

In March 2020, I was injured on the job. It was 4:00 a.m. when I realized the severity of my injury. I could barely move the left side of my body and the pain was never ending. The company doctor diagnosed me with a sprained shoulder and back on the left side. I was prescribed muscle relaxers and anti-inflammatory medication. At 3:00 p.m., I was home alone when I reached to plug in my charger and was consumed with pain that landed me on the floor for the next 12 hours. I spent those hours crying out to God, reevaluating, repenting, and making peace with Him and myself. I declared no more delay, no more pushing people away, and no more walls blocking my blessings. Pride fell to the side and fellowship became a priority in ministry.

In this time of being still, God began to show me myself. By using the nine disciplines, I started on the road of growing closer to God. My faith in Him began to increase. My relationship with Him has become solid. Now, I move without delay. I encourage you to use the nine spiritual disciplines to elevate your faith and trust in God.

Your Sister in Christ,
Trudy Barksdale

Affirmation

I will not allow fear to overwhelm me. I will obey the Lord without delay. I am safe when I am in the perfect will of God. I am victorious.

28

My True Identity

Dear Reader,

I have had many character assassinations in my life. People always looked on the outside and placed judgment on me. I may have acted differently. I may have looked different. I may have communicated differently. As a result, people placed judgement on me that caused me to question my identity.

I had to find out who I am. God created me with leadership characteristics, a quest for knowledge, and confidence. Because I am a female, people misjudged my confidence for masculinity. I am very comfortable in my female body and never wanted to be recognized as a male.

I worked at a chemical plant where there were not many females. There were times when I was the only female and person of color present at planning meetings. I would give input on how to solve a problem only to have it overlooked. However, later in the same meeting, a person would repeat my suggestion and it would be accepted. After a while of going through the same situation, I would stay quiet during the meetings. I felt as if I had to dummy down to get along. I became a silent member because I did not want to be called "the angry black woman." This approach did not help me on my career path.

After my injury, I went to God in prayer. I had to repent because I was not in the place that God wanted me to be. Jeremiah 29:11 (ESV) states, *"For I know the plans I have for you, declares the LORD, plans for welfare and not for evil, to give you a future and a hope."* I meditated on this Scripture and it changed my life. The major thing I changed was my audience. I began to find listeners who valued my input. Now my voice can be heard. I found the place God wanted for me. I learned how to be in locations where I can be appreciated not tolerated. Now, I know the difference.

Your Sister in Christ,
Trudy Barksdale

Affirmation

I will live out the plan God has for me. I will not stay in a place that God wants me to leave. I will not allow my voice to be silenced. I will not allow fear to box me in a pit.

Standing

Dear Reader,

Have you ever felt you were alone? Like the walls were caving in on you? Perhaps you felt like there was no one to turn to for help. Or maybe it felt like you were being smothered, however, you knew you had to stand.

I have been in that place. I remember a time when I had to move and had nowhere to go. However, I knew I had to find somewhere for my four children and I to live. I decided to leave my job for another opportunity that was an hour away. After working there for about nine months, it was time to relocate. I had to leave a place where I was very comfortable that was close to my family.

I became a first-time homeowner in a new area. We moved in just before Christmas. After Christmas, we were hit with a winter storm. We lost power and our water lines froze. Days later when the power was restored, the pipes burst in the ceiling causing $20,000 in damages. I remember standing in the front yard, praying to the Lord for help. I was lost in this situation with no plan. Slowly, the plan began to unfold.

Since I had not changed my children's school, they were able to stay with my parents and continued attending their same school. I stayed with a co-worker who lived nearby so I could be close to my house and monitor the repairs. Additionally, I got to know the couple across the street. This relationship made it easier to transition my children back home. Our relationship has lasted for over twenty years.

This is just one of many situations where I have felt alone. However, the Holy Spirit always puts me in remembrance of the Word of God. The Bible states in Deuteronomy 31:8 (NIV), *"The LORD himself goes before you and will be with you; he will never leave you nor forsake you. Do not be afraid; do not be discouraged."* Try putting your trust in this Scripture the next time you feel alone.

Your Sister in Christ,
Trudy Barksdale

Affirmation

I am an overcomer. I will always pray to the Lord for guidance in all decisions. I will not allow fear to overtake me. I will face all situations head on and not back down. I will trust the plan of God for my life.

The Grief

Dear Reader,

The saddest moment in a parent's life is to hear that their child has died. Those were the words I heard on July 21, 2008. My 15-year-old son, my baby boy, was involved in a car accident. The end result tore at the fibers of my being, pushing me into the safety of God's loving arms.

Everyone grieves differently. I grieved in silence spending numerous nights crying myself to sleep. Yet, I had three other living children depending on me and grieving too. I enrolled in college hoping to dull my pain. I pressed in and completed my degree in three years, but the pain continued.

I heard about the Empty Chair Method for Grief and decided to try it. I placed a chair in front of me, then I visualized my son sitting in the chair. Next, I began to say all the things I wanted to tell him before his death that I had not released. Over time, the Empty Chair Method along with prayer began to lift the grief.

Now, I am enjoying beautiful memories of my son. I am grateful for the time the Lord allowed me to spend with my son. Through my relationship with my son, I learned many things that help me today and have memories that cause me to smile. These are the moments I share with my grandchildren when I tell them about their uncle who they did not have a chance to know.

The Lord is truly with us at all times. He sees and knows everything. When we take the time to learn His character, we will understand His ways. Malachi 3:6 states, *"For I am the LORD, I change not."* Therefore, we can depend on what we know about the Lord.

In conclusion, the death of my son awakened the inner power of healing and manifestation in me. It taught me the power of visualization that brought me to the Loving Arms of God. I now help others suffering from grief to a position of healing.

Your Sister in Christ,
Trudy Barksdale

Affirmation

I will work through the grieving process and allow the love of the Lord to heal me. I will not hold on to my pain because I am not alone. Time will bring peace and love will always win.

No Regret

To Myself:

Have you ever had a dream or desire? Something you wanted to do. Some place you wanted to live. A career you desired to have. When I was younger, I was fascinated by a career with NASA (National Aeronautics and Space Administration). I loved the thought of being in the sky or in outer space.

Not long ago, I attended my first airshow. It was very exciting to me. I watched the aircrafts ascend, descend, twist, and turn as they performed their routines. I was able to see some close up. I was amazed at how the pilots handled them in the air that day.

There was a moment when I noticed the thought of regret entering my mind. I immediately cast down those thoughts of doubt and depression. I refused to give in to the devil. The Bible states in 2 Corinthians 10:5, *"Casting down imaginations, and every high thing that exalteth itself against the knowledge of God, and bringing into captivity every thought to the obedience of Christ."* I began to thank the Lord for the choices I made in life. I know dreams and visions are necessary for life. They ultimately lead to purpose, joy, and fulfillment. Although the journey to self is often filled with question marks and commas, I trust God to order my steps. I have learned to face fear with hope. I know I am safe with God.

There is nothing wrong with having dreams and visions. There's nothing wrong when there is a shift in your life. We should learn to depend on the Lord in everything that we do. As we go through life, we may have a glimpse of the future. However, we don't know the end. Only the Lord knows the end. We must live a life that is pleasing to the Lord and accept His will for our lives.

NASA was my dream, but purpose detoured me to my place of destiny. I AM is ordering and directing my path. I am in good hands with God. I am writing this letter to myself saying, "I have lived a full life and I have lived a life without regrets."

From Trudy Barksdale

Affirmation

I will live my life without regrets. I will not allow the enemy to steal my joy. I will put my trust in the plan God has for me. I will live in peace. I can do all things with Christ.

About the Author

Trudy Barksdale is a servant of the Lord. She has a Bachelor of Science degree in Business Management from Liberty University. She has been certified by the International John Maxwell Team for speaking and coaching. She is a mother of four and a grandmother of seven. She resides in Newport News, Virginia. She is passionate about the things of God. She is a personal growth coach to others seeking help.

As a creative leader, Trudy has an innovative, resilient impact on black women ages 15 to 35 through her team building and problem-solving skills. As a leader, she is always evolving and committed to growth. She creates a safe atmosphere for women to be open about their situations. Afterwards, she works with women on a positive path forward to meet their goals. She believes her actions speak louder than her words. For more information, email TrudyBarksdale@gmail.com.

Letters Written By
Dr. Catherine Coleman

Who Do You Think You Are?

Who do you think you are, learning to love yourself and living life to the fullest?

Who do you think you are, finding beauty and lessons in all junctures of life, miniscule and momentous?

Who do you think you are, manifesting peace in areas of your life once filled with discontent and fear?

Who do you think you are, navigating through trials and opposition as if you are undefeated and unfazed?

Who do you think you are, shining your light all over the cosmos, spreading joy, smiling all bright in harmony with the I AM?

Who do you think you are, no longer making critical decisions based on temporary emotions?

Who do you think you are, putting God first in everything you do, not relying on your own understanding, but solely depending on Him to be your all and all?

Who do you think you are, trusting God's timing,

surrendering to His will, while seeking clarity and understanding?

Who do you think you are, stepping into your purpose while uplifting humanity, finally unperturbed by notions of others?

Who do you think you are, conquering rejection, betrayal, and abandonment despite years of silent mental and emotional battles?

Who do you think you are, forgiving the past, healing childhood wounds, and releasing burdens?

Who do you think you are, running this race with patience, changing course as needed, while developing courage in the process?

Who do you think you are, breaking generational curses, refusing harmful habits and self-sabotaging traits that once ruled your very existence?

Who do you think you are, setting boundaries, honoring your temple despite the awkwardness of finally saying, "no" to familiarity, and "yes" to the will of God concerning you?

Who do you think you are, questioning outdated religious practices, defying the principles of white supremacy, and no longer willing to participate in the repetitious cycles of violence, control, and deception that perpetuate hate and division among the human race?

Who do you think you are, advocating for the voiceless, the less fortunate, and the underprivileged?

Who do you think you are, at peace with yourself and fellow man?

Affirmation

I am complete, fulfilled with the walls of my understanding of myself. Learning to love myself is the most powerful weapon anyone can have. I am who God says I am. I am a weapon of power in the hands of a Mighty God.

Fear of Failure

Dear Fear of Failure,

You no longer have permission to live within my thoughts! I chose prosperity, abundance, and overflow as a mindset and core principle of beliefs. This letter is written as a declaration to remind you to focus your energy and thoughts on God's fullness, joy, favor, and fortune rather than pondering problems and fear of the unknown. Fear of failure only causes agony, mental stress, and emotional weariness.

Declare with me, "I will not feel guilty for believing that I deserve financial prosperity, for it is my heritage." According to John 10:10, Jesus came that we may have life more abundantly. I choose to believe God's Word. Will you trust Him? Proverbs 10:22 (NKJV) states, *"The blessing of the LORD makes one rich, And He adds no sorrow with it."* Also decree the following, "I trust that my spoken words have power and that speaking prosperity affirmations brings forth evidence in my life." Do not be afraid to speak forth prosperous words aloud. Open your mind and heart to believe. It won't always be easy, but remember, you are rewiring your brain to shift into this mindset. Simply let go and trust.

"There is no failure in God," are lyrics that I'm reminded of. You had better believe that gospel music hit different growing up in the 80's. Milton Brunson and The Thompson Community Choir were always in rotation on

WOAD, my mother's radio station of choice, and soon to be second place of employment. It was mid-summer. As a young jerry curl wearing, soon to be third grader, I remember that song bumping in my mom's Nissan Pulsar as she pulled into the parking lot of Voice of Calvary Ministries. Summer camp was on and popping and so was the rubber against her tires in competition with the pebble rocks, and the heat from the pavement that made a smoke just as dry as my curl. For whatever reason, that song aired every single day at the exact same time. The groovy tempo, heavy on the horns, thick on the bass, and lead singer's growl was a skill that I never quite perfected. My interpretation always ended with a scratchy throat, coughing, heavy breathing, needing water. But what captivated my heart strings the most were the convincing delivery of the bridge, *"He'll hear you when you call, catch you before you fall. Just have faith. He'll be right there. There is no failure in God."* Hearing those lyrics today is even more captivating now that I have lived long enough to know, see, and feel God's work in my life. He can't fail; therefore, we have no reason to fear failure or anything else.

When tempted to dwell on limiting beliefs, doubt your abilities, or use negative self-talk, think on God's abundance. Romans 8:28 reassures us that all things are working together for the good because we are called according to His purpose. Allow the following affirmations to enter your conscious and subconscious mind. Repeat them daily and observe the evolution within yourself. Now go forth with confidence…

Defeat fear with faith,
Dr. Catherine

Affirmation

I can do all things through Christ who strengthens me.
My ability to conquer challenges is limitless. My potential to succeed is limitless.
I can achieve all things and am worthy of success.
I am allowed to share value with the world and prosper while doing so.
I give myself permission to succeed. New opportunities are coming my way.
Challenges are opportunities to grow.
I have positive thoughts and a sound mind.
I am enough just as I am.
I have an attitude of gratitude.
I am empowered to fulfill my purpose on earth.
When faced with fears, I am brave.
I have the power to make positive change.
I foster healthy relationships.
I deserve the best that life has to offer.
I make decisions consciously and with clarity. I am in control of my emotions.
I shed limiting beliefs of myself. I am committed to self-growth.
I can be anything I choose to be.

I am open to new ideas and I choose to be happy.

I can achieve whatever I set my sights on.

I am committed to my dreams and I speak to myself with compassion.

I am prosperous, wise, and intuitive.

I am grateful for the abundance I have already received.

Weary and Worn

Dear Catherine,

Go lay down! This letter is written as a reminder that we all need and deserve rest… I wear many hats like most women thriving during the post pandemic era. Many of us acquired more responsibility as a result of personal and or professional matters due to the impact of COVID-19. Our world completely changed, and with that reversal came the evolution of policies, procedures, and protocol for just about every industry within the United States of America. The outcome is that many women have more responsibilities within the workforce now than prior to the transformation of 2020. Working, providing for our families and caretaking while managing so many daunting tasks has added pressure and complexity causing mental, emotional, and even physical decline. Not for all, but for so many. Questionaries and polls reveal that many women are beyond tired; they are completely exhausted. I wonder, what would Jesus do?

As an educator, I've felt the weight of the new era for sure. Regardless of the circumstance, it's only fitting that we thank God for healing our bodies, sustaining us, and keeping us sane throughout the pandemic. He is keeping you and I, and I'm glad about it. It often perplexes me as to how uninformed the general population is regarding teacher salaries and summer breaks. Someone always has an off-topic joke about teachers not having to work

45

during the summer months. My rebuttal is usually, "It would be nice if we only had to work 40 hours a week." Unfortunately, they still don't comprehend how stressful, tiring, and demanding the job can be. But here again, I ponder, what would Jesus do? We have an answer. He rested.

I am reminded of the account in Mark 4 where Jesus went to rest in the boat after teaching His followers that day. As we've been challenged by disaster, so were the disciples. After experiencing strong winds and waves, the disciples woke Jesus, questioning if He cared for them, afraid they would drown. It was that day that His followers witnessed His power and might as He calmed the raging sea by speaking to the winds and waves. In verse 40 He says, "Why are you afraid? Do you still have no faith?"

Could it be that Jesus is posing that same question of us? He is with us, there is no need to fear what lies ahead. Be like Jesus. Let's make time to rest and recover. We have the authority to speak to the challenging forces that come to disrupt our lives. God will always show Himself mighty and strong. Singing, "I'm about to go lay down, I'm about to go lay down."

Self-love wins,
Dr. Catherine Nicole

Affirmation

I am running to the ocean, river, or sea in search of the unity, peace, and joy that I need to be set free. I come for revival and refreshing of the joy and love that is screaming out to me. I am entitled to a revival of heart, mind, body, and soul. Self-love is a requirement for success in life, love, relationships, as well as entrepreneurship in order to accomplish every goal. It is time to rest, relax, and move forward.

Legacy

Dear Legacy,

Girlfriend, you had better pat yourself on the back and acknowledge the growth you've made. Life for Langston's mama may not have been a crystal stair, but the last cycle you've endured was not all dividends, decimals and departures to Dubai either. Destination "Golden Time of Day" arrived later than imagined and with a great cost, although "forty is the new thirty," according to new socially acceptable trends and popular belief. What matters most is that you've learned the required lessons, championed through life's challenges, aligned, and ascended to your rightful place in this world. God has proven His love for you…and it didn't just begin within your season of suffrage. He has been taking care of your people for a long time.

"Serving the Lord will pay off afterwhile," resonates my spirit in a meaningful way now that I've spiritually and emotionally matured. Making the dash to Sunday School during the summer months was an adventure. It had to have been the summer of 1993. The taste of dust in my throat as granny's 60's Chevy collided with overheated pebble rocks and Mississippi clay turned red dust was an indication that we were near granny and paw-paw's church. My granny, Catherine, had been the head usher ever since I could remember. Her pearly white button-down uniform dress matched precisely with her silky

stockings and heavenly white gloves. Riding with granny meant that paw-paw had more than likely been left behind. Regardless, we'd be on time, which meant we parked in her favorite parking space thirty minutes prior to the start of Sunday School. In many instances, the church doors had not been open. Oh, but this Sunday. This one was unlike any other. It was nonidentical to any ever known. Paw-paw was not coming to church…

Morning devotion led by the good deacons at Concord Missionary Baptist Church over in Forest, Mississippi was a sight and sound to behold. Honey child, talk about fear and trembling. Those thunderous testosterone heavy tones of tenor and baritone, baptized with a bar of bass echoed throughout the sanctuary, into the vestibule, across the empty daffodil field, into the over yonder byway. I declare the Gregorian chant reached Heaven. This Sunday, paw-paw was not seated with the deacons. I empathized with granny and sat as close to her as I could. So close that the perfume Aunt Linda had purchased for her the prior Christmas somehow lingered onto my linen dress. As delightful as granny looked and smelled, her countenance never gave way to the emotions she was feeling as a result of my grandfather's behavior. Her good friend, Ms. Margret Glover, whispered in her ear, but not really, "Cat, you look so good. Pat yourself on the back." She cackled in reply, "Really, sho-nuff," as if she didn't have a clue. I knew she was hurting deeply, but the way my granny smiled and strutted around on that burnt red carpet with collection plate in hand, you would have never known that he had packed all his belongings, left her and headed north-north just days ago, the day of her retirement party. It didn't make sense. I contemplated and tried to make sense of what was happening within my pre-adolescent consciousness. What I do know is that this chapter of their love story was my first awareness and lesson on how to cope with rejection and abandonment as a prideful black woman inundated with respect and honor for herself.

Now all of granny's girls could sing. But granny, not so much. You couldn't tell her that. Her starched white collar stood on her neck like a clerical collar on clergy as she belted notes loudly and proudly competing with the deacons during devotion. Bless her heart! She was strong and wrong and all over the scale but not to God's ears. I looked at her just as bewildered as I could be. I smiled because she did—another lesson noted. Happiness is temporary. Let nothing steal your joy! Out of nowhere she mumbled beneath her breath, "Serving the Lord will pay off afterwhile." I didn't know much about love, but I pondered how she could be so angry prior to leaving the house. Yet she sang quite merrily in this moment— another lesson noted. Encourage yourself with words of affirmation loudly and proudly.

"Where is Sue? She should be here by now," she passively aggressively addressed me indirectly. Swiftly picking up the lyrics right where she'd left off. It wasn't hard to rationalize that my mom, Sue, was probably still getting dressed. Besides, my mom had been attending to granny's needs all morning; listening to her repeat "the event" repeatedly, even applying her make-up and sprucing up that sandy blonde wig that Aunt Mary didn't care much for. My granny looked like a million bucks but quickly forgot why—another lesson noted. During your worse moments, dress yourself with purpose and passion. Look your best so you can will yourself to feel even better. Feeling truly is the secret. I knew what granny's question really implied. What she really meant to ask was, "Will Sue get here in enough time, before pastor takes his stance in the pulpit, to sing-preach everybody into a frenzy and make me proud as a peacock."

Suddenly, I heard my mama's keys rattling on the outside of the corridor of closed double doors. Like always, super woman to the rescue, she arrived just in time. My mama sashayed right in those doors speaking to everybody, smiling from ear to ear. She was a local celebrity. In my mind, she was super woman. She kissed granny on the cheek and sat a few pews away from us. If I knew one thing then and now, my mama was always going to be there for granny not in merely words, but in deeds—another lingering life lesson…

Granny never stopped believing and serving God. I'd hear granny curse a little every now and then, but she never stopped praying. She sings loud and proud till this day and still makes demands of my mother, who is her main caretaker. Unfortunately, paw-paw became ill. He summoned granny north-north to aid in nursing him back to health. I don't know if I could have, but granny did just that. I'm convinced that it must have been her prayer and I honored her wishes—another lesson learned. Respect other's wishes without judgement. What a beautiful love story they had. Granny loved him for another thirty years prior to his passing a few years ago.

Thirty years later, I have been graced to reflect on how my grandmother, mother and aunts have navigated this complexity called life. Through war, famine, global pandemic, discrimination, desegregation, health crisis, divorce, loss of loved ones, disease, and day to day struggles, they have persevered. I reflect them and am therefore convinced that everything is working in Divine order, even when I don't understand the purpose nor the outcome. Just as Ms. Margaret encouraged granny all those years ago, I pray that you too can reflect on your journey and pat yourself on the back. I'm grateful for the lessons as I have developed self-awareness and self-love in the process.

Legacy has rewarded this blessed assurance that no matter what occurs in life, serving the Lord pays off afterwhile.

With love,
Dr. Catherine Nicole

Affirmation

I am a gift from God, in season and out of season. I am highly favored and operate with a sound mind at all times. I push, press and win with God. I have learned the power of the gift to applaud myself. I am love.

About the Author

Dr. Catherine Coleman received a Doctorate in the field of Education (EdD.) in Curriculum and Instruction from Jackson State University. She has served as a teacher educator in the Canton Public School System, Canton, MS, and the International Academy of Smyrna, Smyrna, GA. She is currently a teacher/educator at Kipp Vision, Atlanta, GA.

She is the former Director of Kids Kollege Freedom School and an Adjunct Professor at Jackson State University. She has received numerous awards in the field of Education.

Dr. Coleman is an entrepreneur, mentor, and advocate for children and adults. She is the Founder and owner of Crowned in Royalty, LLC and the Crowned in Royalty Academy. Crowned in Royalty serves as a social service outreach dedicated to addressing the educational, emotional, and social needs of children and families. The Crowned in Royalty Online Boutique financially supports the mission and goal of improving the lives of children and families.

She is a Co-Anchor on the Mother Daughter Show that runs daily on PIC TV.

Her works include What It Takes To Rebuild A Village After Disaster: Stories From Internally Displaced Children and Families of Hurricane Katrina and Their Lessons to Our Nation and her latest body of work, the second edition of Mama's Book of Prayers: Prayers, Prompts, Power & Praise Journal and Workbook released in June 2023.

Letters Written By Dawn Dean

Little Boys and Girls

Dear Little Boys and Girls,

I'm sorry someone hurt you. I'm sorry no one was there to protect or console you. I'm sorry you weren't allowed to express your feelings. I'm sorry you weren't shown love or given hugs. I'm sorry you didn't have a hot meal or a warm bed to comfort you. I'm sorry you didn't have both parents to support and raise you. I'm sorry you were bullied by bullies who were bullied themselves. I'm sorry you've had to carry such a weighted burden yourself.

Blessings on you,
Dawn Dean

Affirmation

I am no longer allowing my childhood to dictate my future. I am being transformed for greatness in spite of and because of all I have been through. I am determined.

Young Ladies and Men

Dear Young Ladies and Men,

I am delighted you have faced your fears. I am delighted you've found people who care. I am delighted you are happy and healed. I am delighted to see your light shine from within. I am delighted you made a choice to forgive. I am delighted you live by God's will. I am delighted the sun's warmth hugs you from above. I am delighted you have the capacity to love.

Faithfully yours,
Dawn Dean

<u>Affirmation</u>

I am empowered to walk in the light of a new day. I have been weaponized to win.

Trauma

Dear Trauma,

It's been a long battle, but I am determined to win. You've led me down many painful roads and dark avenues, planting doubt, traps, and sinful things. Our first encounter severely traumatized me as a kid. Each year, you gripped tighter, disrupting my adolescent and youthful adult years.

Trauma, you've robbed me over and over again. At one point in time, you confiscated my joy, hope and dreams. So much so, I could no longer sincerely grin. So, I created a smiley mask and learned how to pretend. I pretended to be happy while my spirit frowned and bared.

Daily, you spoke negativity into my mind and told lies I would come to believe. You'd say things like, "You are useless and unworthy of love. Your life has no meaning or purpose." All those ugly words destroyed me bit by bit.

You subtracted my self-worth, deleted my self-value and lowered my self-esteem. You made me retreat to a place of make-belief, I called Imaginary Island. There, as a wiser mature woman, I found solace through creative writing.

Within my sadness and wounds, I discovered your purpose, Trauma. You weren't there to taunt me or be a burden. I came to see the bigger picture for my struggles

and problems. I uncovered God's plan, hope renewed, and dreams began to flourish. Time began to close old wounds and you slowly diminished.

Gratefully, I thank God for your existence. I now can genuinely smile and love the reflection of me. Though healing trauma is an ongoing journey, what has healed allows me to inspire other boys, girls, men, and women to overcome adversity to win.

Yours truly,
Dawn Dean

Affirmation

I am free from doubt and fear. I am an unstoppable force of energy and strength.

God's Plan

Dear Reader,

Today, as an adult, I stand with my eyes to the sky. I walk with Jesus, the Holy Spirit. I am blessed by a Mighty God.

I've forgiven those who have trespassed as enemies. I have healed and learned to repress past mental, physical, and environmental trauma. They no longer reside here.

The journey was long, lonely, and depressed. It was what it was; a seraphic guide to my purpose.

Sincerely,
Dawn Dean

Affirmation

I am divinely promoted to be healed as well as to forgive. I am moving forward in love.

Knowing the Power of SELF

I AM SELF-reflecting:
Loving the person that I see.

I AM coming to know mySELF:
Whose and who I am in Christ.

I AM SELF-aware:
Mindful of my strengths and areas of lack.

I AM SELF-assured:
SELF-confident in my skills and talents abundantly
    stacked.

I AM SELF-empowered:
Onward, I will not revert back.

I AM SELF-sufficient:
Trusting the process and God's will and plan.

I AM SELF-study:
Open-minded and learning new things about mySELF.

I AM SELF-believing:
I possess the power to defeat enemies when attacked.

For I AM endowed by the Word of God:
He protects and guides me.

About the Author

 Dawn Dean is a five-time published author, wellness coach, and mental health advocate. She's co-authored a poetry book and raised funds for mental health awareness. She is also the founder of the self-empowerment wellness blog sisterslikeus.com and the creative director of the Sisters Like Us Win brand (@sisterslikeuswin).

Dawn began rebuilding her life and coaching business after succumbing to chronic illnesses and depression. She realized the importance of self-care and overall well-being and now coaches and speaks on the importance of mental, physical, spiritual, and environmental health.

Though Dawn learned the hard way, health is wealth, she's discovered her life's purpose and how her stories and words can motivate others to live well.

When Dawn isn't writing, coaching, or learning how the mind, brain and body cohesively operate, she's producing self-empowerment courses, books, and journals, and creating memorable moments with her three children and grandkids in Northern Virginia.

Contact: DawnDeanBooksandFilm@gmail.com

Letters Written By Nitza M. Diaz

Trust God, Love, and Wait on God

My Dear Victoria,

Never forget to trust God, love, and wait on God!

You are the unexpected miracle of God that made my secret desires become reality. You are wise beyond the age of five. You are the gift that confounds the wise. Your grasp of the Word of God is mesmerizing. You are the heart and hand of God's creation. I am so blessed to be a mother of such an amazing little girl.

Many years before your birth, I told a friend I always wanted to have a daughter. Her response was, "That's nice. I will write it down in my prayer journal." Ten years later, at the age of 44, God decided it was time for you to come. You are a miracle from God. You caused doctors to scratch their heads in wonderment and made them question their science. You epitomize all things are possible with God. God is God, and He does as He pleases.

People made me question and sometime doubt if you

would be born healthy. The echoes of words, "You're too old. The baby will not be healthy," stole the joy of the first trimester of my pregnancy. I allowed fear to diminish my faith. But the God in me stayed faithful. Nine months later, my beautiful Victoria, you were born. Holding you for the first time solidified that when we trust God and wait on His promises, miracles happen. Learn from my experience and don't listen to others who are always ready to tell you that miracles do not happen. If you serve and love God, He will always bless you!

You are my miracle! You are my blessing! When I saw your smile and perfect features, I cried because I could not grasp how much God loves me and how much He utterly understands that I truly needed you in my life. I allowed the fear of the unknown to make me depressed and not trust His process of waiting. I waited 10 years for you to come. My love always trusts and knows that God is for you. All things are possible with God. Never underestimate the power of God, who makes the impossible possible!

Victoria, I love you from infinity and beyond!

Your thankful mother,
Nitza

Affirmation

I will not underestimate the power of God to make anything possible. I trust the God of the impossible to work miracles in my life!

Nothing is Impossible When We Believe

To the Moms Who Believe That Their Babies are Not Going to Make It:

My daughter, Victoria, was born healthy in 2017. A week later, I noticed her breathing was labored. I called the pediatrician and made an appointment to make sure it was nothing dangerous.

The pediatrician said her oxygen level was low. Still, she comforted me by making me believe that her oximeter was not working and told me to take her to the emergency department. As soon as I arrived, the nurses took her from my arms. I watched the nurses and doctors attach a breathing machine. I watched tubes being placed in her nose and needles in her little arms. I was terrified, yet all I could do was watch and wait.

My daughter was admitted to the hospital, and after many tests that night, the doctors still could not tell me her diagnosis. I felt so helpless. I was waiting for something that hopefully would ease my mind and increase my faith. Who was I waiting on? Was I waiting on the doctors to have the final say? Was I waiting on myself to have enough faith to expect a miracle? Was I waiting on the Lord?

No, I WAS NOT waiting on the Lord. I was waiting for a medical provider to tell me that my baby daughter would be leaving the hospital healthy.

During my waiting, a specialist came into the room and told me that even though they could not offer a concrete diagnosis, they could assure me they did not know if my baby would make it. She was on a ventilator, and every time they tried lowering the amount of oxygen the baby was receiving, her body was not able to handle it. She could not breathe without the ventilator. Here I was, waiting on a doctor for a solution, and in this waiting, all I got were words of death.

That night, I told God I was calling on an army of believers to believe in faith for her miracle. I was upset at God because I thought my waiting for Him had to be on my terms. God is God, and we need to humble ourselves and let Him do what only God can do.

It was at this moment that I asked for forgiveness for my unbelief. I prayed for forgiveness for my faithlessness. I prayed for forgiveness for trying to tell God what to do.

Suddenly, I received a text message from a friend who told me all the band members at his son's university had stopped playing and told the audience to pray for a baby who was extremely sick. Imagine a stadium full of people watching a homecoming with a band praying for my baby. Wow, if that was not God showing me love, what was He showing me? I only knew one person in that stadium praying for my daughter. I did not know anyone else. God showed me how much favor exists in my life. He showed me that nothing is impossible when we believe.

Now ask yourself: Am I genuinely waiting on the Lord? Do I want God to show off His love in a miraculous manner? Who am I trusting?

God does God, and we follow. God always wants the best for us. I know it sounds cliché, but I was not waiting on Him. I did not trust Him. He loved me so much that He had people in a stadium at a University praying for a baby they did not know!

From a Mother Full of Faith

<u>Affirmation</u>

I trust God with the impossible because when I am going through a desert and emotionally feel as though nothing is going to change, that is when God's powers are manifested. In the desert is where He provides me with an oasis to rest. I love the God of the impossible.

You are Good Enough

To the Women Who Believed the Label "You ARE NOT GOOD ENOUGH":

For the women who believe:

- ✓ Your skin is not good enough
- ✓ Your hair is not good enough
- ✓ Your English is not good enough
- ✓ You are NOT GOOD enough

I was like you. I believed the lies that I was not good enough! I believed that I could not achieve it because I was not good enough!

One day God asked me, "Why do you think you are not good enough?"

I said, "God, I don't know why I believed the lies. God, how can I be good enough if I don't have what it takes to be good enough?"

God said, "Tell Me, daughter, what does not being good enough mean? Why are you not good enough?"

I could not answer His question. I cried! I could not concretely explain why I was not good enough. I cried out, "God, please free me from these beliefs! I want to be free!"

God said, "Nitza, I will make you stronger!"

"I think I know that, God," I said.

"Really, but do you believe it?" He asked.

"I don't know if I believe or trust you, God," was my reply.

"When have I not been with you during your struggles? Your challenges? Your peaks and valleys? When have I left you? I never left. I am still here for you. I protect you! Let it go and rest in me," He commanded.

I don't know or will never understand why I thought I was not good enough, but I know God loves me and His favor is upon my life.

Woman, remove that not-good-enough label from yourself! So easy yet so hard to do, and I believe that:

- ✓ You are loved
- ✓ You matter
- ✓ You are valued
- ✓ You are good enough!

From an Ex-Believer of the Label "You ARE NOT GOOD ENOUGH"

Affirmation

Whenever I hear "you are not good enough," I will stop! Breathe three times! Look up because God says, "YOU ARE GOOD ENOUGH! You are the apple of My eye. My crafted Masterpiece given to the world."

I am more than enough. I am who God says I am. I am the proud daughter of I AM.

To All of Those Pastor Kids Who Grew Up with Unnecessary Rules That Religion Created

Dear Pastor Kids (PKs),

I write this letter to the ones who survived the journey of growing up at the intersection of faith, religiosity, and family. This intersection can make us grow up in that shadow of "sacred devotion." But what if you grew up with that sacred devotion mainly to bear witness to a community's shallow emotions? Or what if this holy devotion came with eyes watching every step we made or ears listening to every word we uttered? What if this sacred devotion had heavy, illogical, and absurd expectations?

Was this all worth it? I don't know. I do know we have dreams, passions, and an identity in Christ that is not part of our parents' identity.

Let me tell you part of my story. I grew up in Puerto Rico in an evangelical family. I come from a family of pastors. My great-grandmother founded an evangelical denomination. Having a great-grandmother as an evangelical in the 1900s was rare in Puerto Rico because, at that time, Catholicism was the dominant religion. Nonetheless, my parents were born evangelical, and thus, all the children grew up not knowing what Catholicism was or was not. I remember feeling alienated from some

of my classmates because they went to Catholic festivals I was not allowed to attend. Their religion seemed fun. My religion and my position as a PK seemed dull and harsh.

Furthermore, I learned the rules of what it meant to behave and act like a PK. People believe that our behavior is to be an example for others. We could not walk without being watched. We could not talk without having others hear. We could not express our humanity. We were to be some kind of saint figure and nothing else. It was hard to be what others thought I should be. Watching other children act free in the church was frustrating; I could not.

During my many traumatizing years, I will never forget that I was very frustrated about religiosity (I know now what it is called. As a child, I could not articulate it), so I took the scissors and cut my hair short. When my parents saw me, they said nothing except that I could not go to church with a haircut like that. Hence, I stayed and did not go. This religious incident of religiosity broke my spirit because I could not understand why cutting one's hair was a sin for women. I stayed home until my hair grew long enough for church members not to notice.

After that incident, I did not want to be part of a system that showed no mercy or love. If Jesus was about love and the one commandment He left us was to love God with all my heart, mind, and strength and to love my neighbor as myself, why was this religion that professed God's love for us not practicing it? I hated driving to that

small church. I hated seeing the members. I hated their looks. I hated everything that resembled what they stood for. All I heard was: *"We don't date. We can't go to the movies and sit beside sinners, except if it is a movie about Jesus during Easter. Alcohol is from the devil. Smoking is a sin and it will kill you. Dancing is giving into temptation. If Jesus returned and you were doing any of these things, you would go to hell."* These comments and prohibitions created more trauma and resentment toward the loving God I thought I knew.

I grew up traumatized by the religious fanatics who claimed to know a God who loves them but not the ones like me. It was one of the most challenging spaces to be in. I felt conflicted and torn because I love God and who He is, but I could not love people like them. As I was growing up, I would try to understand this type of hypocrisy, but I always ended up angry at this religion.

I went to college and I felt freedom. Hey, I pierced my ears and put on jeans and some make-up. I went home and was scared, but my parents were not upset at any of these things.

During this journey, I have learned that:

- My identity is not only about being a PK. I have a name, different personality, characteristics, likes, and dislikes.
- Whenever I felt that the spotlight was often shining my way, ALL I did was EMBRACE IT!

<u>YOU CAN DO ALL THINGS THROUGH CHRIST WHO GIVES YOU STRENGTH!</u>

- Find comfort in the love and guidance of our Lord Jesus Christ.
- Find strength and unity in the moments you spend with God and your family.
- Support your parents in the assignment that they have from God.
- Share God's love and compassion with those who are weary, faithless, and hopeless.

May the Lord Jesus Christ continue to give you strength and courage to complete your mission on earth.

Yours truly,
Nitza M. Diaz

Affirmation

My role as a PK is part of God's plan. The pain, the tears, the loneliness, and the criticisms teach me to have the joy, love, peace, and trust God gives me.

I am strong in Him. His grace is sufficient for me. I am not a mistake. God takes care of me! I am beautiful because I am fearfully and wonderfully made.

I will trust Him. I will find joy. I am wonderful. I am strong in the Lord. I am wonderfully and faithfully made. I am loved. He cares about me.

An "Ode" to Rosita Where the Sun Shined Too Bright

Dear Rosita,

Your love for your children is a strong and beautiful bridge that crossed from Honduras to the United States to chase a dream sold to you for $20,000. You knew that when your husband was killed, it was time to leave, and with all your strength, you took your children and walked over 1,000 miles to reach a dream that never was.

You watched your children go hungry, cry, suffer, and even dehydrate to escape a world full of darkness, violence, and chaos. You left for Diego and Elena, who came into this world, not knowing that one day they had to cross a bridge to the unknown. While in the desert, you had so little food, all you could think about was how close death was running behind. You spent three days in the desert feeding your children tablespoons of cold white rice. You had no water. However, you had strength, love, and a dream for a better life.

When you finally reached the town in Mexico where the Coyote was waiting, your eyes shone and your smile was as bright as a star during those romantic summer nights. You finally got to the dirty motel, infested with roaches and mice, but more importantly, full of people waiting to get to "promise land." A couple of hours later, the Coyote arrived at the motel. He wore a nice tuxedo

to help you cross the border that was full of dirt, sadness and poverty.

You walked and walked and walked some more until the Coyote told you that you now had to go inside the trunk of the car so no one could find you. The Coyote had paid a border guard to let them cross without any trouble. You crossed the bridge toward the dreams of a better life. However, you could not see the strong and beautiful bridge because you were in the darkness.

The Coyote stopped the car, opened the trunk, and helped you and the children out of the trunk. You looked and intuitively knew that you had crossed! The air was fresh, the flowers more vibrant. Rosita, you accomplished what you set out to do. You were going after that dream full of opportunities.

The Coyote dropped you off at the designated motel to wait for your uncle. You were finally going to fulfill your dream to provide your children with what they deserve. You went to the motel room and slept. You jumped like a little girl excited for a new adventure the next day. You had breakfast! You were waiting for your uncle when you suddenly heard: "Everyone get up! This is the ICE (Immigration and Customs Enforcement) raid! Please show us your passports or any form of identification." You froze but complied. The officer took your children and told you to walk in the opposite direction. You ran towards your children and gave them a kiss. You screamed at your older child to take care of the younger one. Your dream vanished. Your nightmare began. Did you travel for nothing? Did you believe that a nightmare could turn into a dream? Did you know that your kids would be taken away from you? Did you know that the strong and beautiful bridge was an illusion about a dream that did not exist?

Rosita, my heart aches for you. My compassion and love for you cannot bring you to your children right now. Only Jesus can do that. Rosita, I cannot tell you to stay strong because nothing for you matters anymore and no one can know your pain. No husband, no children! Rosita, please trust God. The only one who knows and understands your pain is God who gave up His son for you. God understands what sacrificial love is all about.

Rosita, I pray that you embrace God. I pray that you know that I am here for you. I pray that His peace fills you up and that you talk to Him about it in those dark moments. I love you!

Rosita, your children wrote this small poem for you:

Your love is a big beautiful rainbow.
When you hug me, a tsunami of love drowns me.
Your smile is as beautiful as the sun's rays of light.
Its blinding light stops me in my tracks.
You are as awesome as can be.
Your hair is a beautiful red-brown, like a fox.
Your skin is a perfect dark tan, like the sand of the
    beaches back home.
You're the best! I love you!

Grace be to you,
Nitza M. Diaz

Affirmation

God loves me! He does not fail! I am protected. I am at peace during chaos. I rejoice in the suffering because He takes care of me. I am strong in the Lord. He fights my battles. There is no giant that He cannot destroy. God is my rock and my provider. No weapon formed against me shall prosper. I will see my children again because I see the goodness of the Lord!

About the Author

 Nitza M. Diaz is an Education Consultant with the State Education Resource Center and the CT Parent Information and Resource Center. In this role, Nitza provides coaching, professional development, training, and technical assistance for educators, families, community organizations, and faith-based leaders in areas of family engagement, equity, special education, and multilingual learners.

Nitza is a co-lead Consultant for the African-American/Black and Puerto Rican/Latino Curriculum, a course of study to be offered as an elective option to high schoolers statewide in the 2022-23 school year grams as a result of Public Act 19-12 passed in May 2019. Nitza has been the lead Consultant for the Puerto Rican/Latino "side" of the state-developed curriculum.

Nitza has provided many professional development sessions on social justice, focusing on socio-cultural instructional strategies that reflect the students being served in the district. Her numerous presentations on social equity, bilingual education, and best practice for multi-lingual students within the community, state, and national levels have been well received by all. She not only shares her learning and experiences with her school, but she also finds the time to interact with diverse communities of learners and teachers. In these communities, she promotes reflection; she is quick to point out strengths and constructively provides tips for strengthening areas that need improvement in the schools and districts.

Nitza holds a B.A. Degree (1995) from Mount Holyoke College, a Master's in Public Health, and a Master of Arts from the University of Connecticut. She will continue her doctoral studies in the fall.

Letters Written By
Dr. Keisha Fleming

Brown Skinned Girl

Dear Brown Skinned Girl,

Keep going! Life will be filled with the good and bad, but you are graced to move forward and be the fierce queen that God has created you to be. The trials you face will awaken the true purpose of your being. Take the limitations off yourself, life is what you create, and it all begins with one idea. You are important to God and He cares about every detail of your life. He cares about your disappointments, blessings, and collects every tear that you shed. Allow the Father to restore the brokenness of your heart and spirit, for He is close to the brokenhearted and saves those who are crushed in spirit. The things that happened to you happened for you! Although you may be scrutinized or ridiculed for your melanated skin, just know that you are one of a kind. Even when the odds are against you, you continue to flourish into the best version of yourself.

Give yourself permission to heal from the pain of losing loved ones. Give yourself permission to honor your loss in a personal way. Give yourself permission to look to the future and birth purpose. Give yourself permission to honor and love yourself. Continue to heal the wounds and prepare for the things that are coming.

You are loved and worthy of love. The life lessons, struggles, and discrimination produced opportunities for growth and success. When you get weary, keep going…you are a true gem and you are enough!

I love you, sister, and I'm always rooting for you!

Love,
KD Fleming

Affirmation

I am smart, witty, beautiful, educated, determined, God-fearing, and I deserve the BEST!

#MeToo

Dear #MeToo,

I joined the military with the core values—honor, courage, and commitment—indoctrinated repeatedly throughout basic school and into the fleet. I was expected to uphold these core values in all that I did, in personal, professional, and even spiritual life. One day, the values that I believed in were stolen without my consent and this event tainted my view of the military forever. The experience haunted me for years because I always blamed myself for "it" happening to me. Out of shame, I didn't tell my family, chain of command, or my closest friends.

How could I let this happen? Should I have fought back? Should I have reported him? These and many more questions circulated through my mind of what I could have done differently. The only fact that remained is "it" happened and now I had to deal with it.

I masked the rage and shame by displaying a smile and using things to fill the voids. The unspoken pain became debilitating and began to show in my daily encounters. The vibrant young lady who was full of promise transformed into a depressed introvert in survival mode. I wanted to come forward but didn't want to be stigmatized because of the trauma. The fear of retaliation affected my sense of trust, safety, and well-being. I felt fear, guilt, and anxiety each time I saw him. My story was never told to my chain of command, but now I have the courage to speak about the injustice I faced. My torment ended when I transitioned to a new duty station, but the brokenness lingered within my soul.

One in four female veterans and one in one hundred male veterans have reported military sexual trauma to Veteran Affairs. One important thing I had to understand was that I was a survivor.

It's not your fault, I'm sorry this happened to you, you are not alone, and YOU ARE A SURVIVOR THAT WILL THRIVE!

Sincerely,
KD Fleming

<u>Affirmation</u>

I am prepared and I have the capacity to receive the blessings for which I have prayed.

Love

Dear Love,

I am ready for you. I have read that you are patient, are kind, do not envy, do not boast, are not proud, do not dishonor others, are not self-seeking, are not easily angered, and keep no record of wrongdoing. God is love and His love is everlasting!

I've freely given you to others, but you were not reciprocated to me. In this, I've had the opportunity to be truthful about myself and the failed relationships from my past. I thought of love as the jitters I would get when a certain person entered a room or the familiar scent of fragrance that reminded me of good times. I've learned love is interconnected to my purpose of existence. Dr. Myles Monroe says, "When purpose is not known, abuse is inevitable." I was lacking the capacity to receive love that I longed for but freely gave. The hurt from my past created a space to harbor distrust, anger, and not forgive the other party. All the things that I read about LOVE were not visible in my life.

It wasn't easy to forgive but it was necessary, even though my flesh felt otherwise. I desire LOVE in every being of my essence and encounter with others. My unforgiveness was only hurting me and not the other person. For a very long time, I was so lost in the hustle of everyday life that I questioned, "WHY ME!" I struggled financially, spiritually, mentally, and physically;

until I FORGAVE! Forgiveness isn't always easy but it's necessary!

Now, I embrace every moment—the good, bad, and ugly because it's creating a beautiful masterpiece. I am the masterpiece and I've given myself permission to live, laugh and most of all LOVE!

LOVE, I AM NOW READY!

Yours truly,
KD Fleming

<u>Affirmation</u>

I give myself permission to forgive, heal, and evolve to my higher self.

Mama and Daddy

Dear Mama and Daddy,

If I could turn back the hands of time, I would have hugged you longer at the airport, called more often, took more trips, and spent more time. I miss you beyond words but thank you for raising me to be the woman that I am today.

I wonder how different my life would have been if you were still here. My life changed forever on that snowy February evening. A strange voice answered the call when I received news that you were involved in an accident at work. Things went dark. I was hundreds of miles away from home, no one to console my cries and ease my fears. All I had left were memories of the man who once protected and provided for his family. Daddy, you were gone and I never got to say goodbye to you. You went to work like you had done for the past 25 years but that day you never came home…this was one of the toughest events I ever had to face. Many questions flooded my thoughts: How? Why my Daddy? You taught me to never question God, but deep inside I didn't understand "why" this was happening.

Mama, eleven years later you went to the doctor for a routine procedure and never came home. I thought we had more time. We had so many plans and so much to do. Thank you for caring for my son while I was in the military, teaching me how to be a "lady," and ensuring that I was able to take care of myself. You were the matriarch of our family, the glue that held everyone together, and now you were gone.

For a long time, I was not ok, but I had enough faith to believe that I would be. I had to be patient with the process and allow myself to be venerable to heal.

Mama and Daddy, I honor your lives and I hope you are proud of me. I incorporate the values I was taught despite the adversity I've faced. Your legacy will live on through your children, grandchildren, and generations to come.

Love and miss y'all beyond words!

Your daughter,
KD Fleming

Affirmation

I give myself permission to adjust my crown and let go of past failures, fumbles and disappointments.

Future Husband

Dear Future Husband,

Every morning, I say a prayer of thanks to God for you. He is a faithful and majestic God, and He has never let me down. He has blessed me with someone like you as a testament of His great love for me. Someone who will love me for who I am and help me cultivate as a person. You are the love of my life, my protector, my king, my lover, and my husband. I pray that your heart is tender towards me and each day you are equipped with greater wisdom, joy, love, and encouragement.

Although we have not met in the capacity of husband and wife, I know you are near. I look forward to many last firsts with you and waking up to your handsome face. I know that any issue we encounter only strengthens our union. I pray against any temptation that distracts you from your purpose and that you are free from the bondages of your past that stagnate your future. It's only a matter of time that I will be in your arms, and I know God has tailor made you just for me.

God, when he is overwhelmed with the world, let him remember Psalm 27:1 so he won't be fearful. Let him be rooted and grounded in love according to Ephesians 3:17.

Future husband, thank you for completely changing and upgrading my life, in ways inside and out. Thank you for sharing the intimate parts of your life with me. I look

forward to the times when we will pray together, build together, and love together!

Until we meet…

Your future wife,
KD Fleming

<u>Affirmation</u>

I give myself permission to RECLAIM my time, CLAP for myself, PROTECT my peace, LOVE without regrets, and KEEP SHINING!

About the Author

Keisha Fleming is an educator, mentor, veteran, minister, and advocate for her community. She earned a BS in Elementary Education from Southern University, M.Ed in Educational Leadership from Louisiana State University, PhD in Christian Counseling from C Squared Education/Day Spring Christian University. Keisha has 16 years of teaching experience and is currently an Assistant Principal. She is a veteran of United States Navy where she served eight years as a Firecontrolman Technician. She desires to continually educate and inspire the students and their families that she encounters. In her professional career, she was recognized as Elementary Teacher of the Year, advocates with Stand for Children, Leaders of Color, Power Coalition SheLeads Alum and is a proud member of Delta Sigma Theta Sorority, Inc., and she serves as the Co-coordinator of the Social Action Committee, and Secretary of the Redistricting Cohort for Louisiana. She is a member of Choice International Family Outreach Worship Center in LaPlace, LA under the leadership of Bishop-Prophet Antoine Jasmine.

Keisha has a strong passion to educate future generations to assist them in becoming a well-rounded

and productive citizen. Throughout the course of her career, she's had opportunities to teach, create curriculums, accommodate multiple intelligences, and bring a hands-on approach to learning. Her greatest strengths include advocating, teaching, motivating, and engaging others to become the best version of themselves.

Keisha lives in Louisiana with her son, Dre, who is currently serving in the Marine Reserves as an Aviation Mechanic.

You can contact Dr. Keisha Fleming on social media (Facebook or Instagram) or via email at madampresidentllc@gmail.com.

Letters Written By
Pamela Grant

I Am a Proverbs 31 Woman

Dear Reader,

As a child and well into my adulthood, I felt I had no value and wasn't good enough. There were times I had a hard time building relationships with people because of childhood scars that left me feeling unwanted.

After years of struggling with low self-esteem, God, in His perfect timing, took me through a season of transformation. He renewed my mind from low self-esteem to being confident that I have value. I have not overcome all my past issues, but God has proven to me He has not forgotten about me and I do have purpose for His Kingdom. He said He just needed me to be a hidden figure while He perfected me in the shadows. His plans are for me to prosper, to give me hope and a future. From that I began to know "who I am." That word of promise ignited me to trust God completely and I began to be transformed more into His image.

I knew I had purpose from reading God's Word. He

said in Psalm 139 that I Am fearfully and wonderfully made and I Am a Proverbs 31 woman. Understanding those words from God, I know through the eyes of God I have value and I Am enough and there is nothing the nay sayers can do about it. I believe what God says!

God has confirmed to me that He has equipped and empowered me for His purpose. He said, "My daughter, you have been faithful and diligently serving My Kingdom in various capacities to win souls for the Kingdom and empowering them individually and collectively to reach their potential for My purpose."

Being a first-time co-author was never something I imagined. This confirms God has greater in store for those who love Him and are obedient to His Will. I encourage you to spend time with God through prayer, seeking His Will for your life. In this season, God has given you and I the opportunity to step out in boldness and confidence to go beyond anything we can imagine. With Him the impossible can be achieved!

Renewed and transformed,
Pamela

Affirmation

I Am a first-time co-author. I Am fearfully and wonderfully made. I Am more than enough. I Am equipped and empowered for purpose. I Am transformed by the renewing of my mind for greater. I Am confident in who I Am.

The Rhythms of Marriage

Dear Hubby,

This inspiration for marriages is dedicated to you.

One day you asked me, "How do we keep the music playing?" Being newlyweds at the time, it was a deep thought question that we didn't know how to answer. Through the years, our marriage has hit some bumpy roads, some we didn't know if we could recuperate from. That question became relevant as the seasons of our marriage began to change and the question "How do we keep the music playing?" needed answers.

Marriage is like RHYTHM—regular, alternating, progressive, flowing, and random. They all come into play as years of marriage accumulate. To God be the glory, we figured out the rhythm of the music we had to play through every seasonal change we've encountered. God is the center of our joy and the conductor of the music that is orchestrated in our hearts. Jesus is the rhythm and melodies we dance to in our hearts for better or worse, for richer or poorer, in sickness and in health. Jesus is the music that keeps the rhythm of life in our marriage to love and to cherish till death do us part. As words of encouragement to married couples, let these words make music in your hearts as you go through the rhythms of your marriage and ask yourselves, "How are we going to keep the music playing?"

When there is INDIFFERENCE, sing rhythms of LOVE. When there is UNHAPPINESS, sing rhythms of JOY. When there is CONFLICT, sing rhythms of PEACE. When there is IMPATIENCE, sing rhythms of SELF-CONTROL. When there is UNKINDNESS, sing rhythms of GENTLENESS. When there is MISTRUST, sing rhythms of FAITH and listen for Gods musical sounds of wisdom. THIS IS HOW WE KEEP THE MUSIC PLAYING.

Hubby, as we head towards 40 years of marriage on the journey God has predestined for us, I love and thank God for you and I'm enjoying the music we make together.

We sing and dance to the rhythms of HALLELUJAH.

Love,
Your Wife

Affirmation

I Am a rhythm maker. I Am committed to my marriage. I Am a faithful wife. I Am trustworthy. I Am a worshipper. I Am grateful. I Am blessed to be called Mom. I Am a legacy builder. I Am an encourager to my family.

Gatekeeper Mindset

Dear Reader,

I have experienced many trials in my life. Like some of us, I didn't think I was going to receive healing nor deliverance. My mind was a gate keeper of thoughts and unforgiveness I had to release. As an introvert, I struggled with communicating and would not join in conversations that had more than three people including myself. With this barrier, I moved in silence accepting what others would say and do.

Being shy, I was being tortured from the inside. This torture silenced me to having no voice and I wouldn't communicate my thoughts and feelings which caused me to fade into the background. Growing up, when activities included teams, the other kids had their popular picks. I was always the last to be picked. I had unresolved issues from my childhood that followed me into adulthood leaving me with a mentality of feeling "not good enough." My introvert personality impacted my life tremendously and I felt worthless, unwanted and neglected.

I was a gatekeeper of thoughts of how others treated me and how some things turned out in my life, blaming others for my childhood issues. I wasn't aware that I had to let go and forgive my past that was keeping me in bondage to be healed of old wounds. I was guilty of holding grudges within myself. Then I met Jesus.

My life began to evolve in a different direction as I let God be the pilot of my life. I met my husband in church and through him I learned the difference between religious and a relationship with Christ. As I grew in my relationship with Christ and obedience, God began to heal me. God spoke to me saying I had to let my past go and I can do all things through Him because He's going to give me the strength.

To fast forward from being an introvert, I have overcome that personality tremulously. God has truly blessed and equipped me for the purpose He created me for.

Glory to God,
Pamela Grant

Affirmation

I Am victorious. I Am no longer hidden. I Am fulfilling my purpose. I Am an overcomer. I Am capable of holding meaningful conversations. I Am walking in destiny. I Am a lover of Jesus Christ.

Gatekeeper Mindset Set Free

Dear Reader,

As I grew in my Christian walk, God set me free from my gatekeeper mindset and manifestations started taking place. I became a servant of Christ sincerely from my heart. God began to unfold and clean me from inside. He removed the negative thoughts I carried within the depths of my mind, not only about people that mistreated and abused me but also the doubts and insecurities I had about myself.

God told me I was healed and set free from the clutches of what the devil was trying to hold me in bondage for. The devil didn't want me to forgive my enemies because he peeked into what God has purposed for me. He knew nothing would be fulfilled through me for God's Kingdom if I carried unforgiveness in my heart. God reminded me of what was penned in His Word about unforgiveness. He said in Mark 11:25-26 (NKJV), *"And whenever you stand praying, if you have anything against anyone, forgive him, that your Father in heaven may also forgive you your trespasses. But if you do not forgive, neither will your Father in heaven forgive you your trespasses."*

I have not dotted every "I" nor crossed every "T" so I asked my Father to forgive me where I sinned as well as forgave myself. By His Word, I learned He loves me and I must trust Him as He leads and navigates my life. I must stand strong in my faith and never waver. It took several years to reach a pivotal point of peace. When you read my profile, you will see how God has transformed my life from my past of an introvert personality. He gave me a voice and worth.

God's grace and mercy abounds for us all. What trauma are you dealing with that the devil has you bound? What do you need to be healed and set free from for your Kingdom purpose to be fulfilled? TO GOD BE THE GLORY for the great things He has and is doing in my life and your life as you heal.

Grace be to you,
Pamela Grant

Affirmation

I Am healed and set free. I Am destined for greater. I Am secure in myself. I Am a positive thinker. I Am a leader. I Am looking up not down.

God Winks

Dear Reader,

There are seasonal changes in our lives that encounter valley and mountain top experiences. In the valley, we have regrets, remorse, confusion, anguish, grief, and emotional destruction. On the mountain top, we rejoice, dance, and are full of laughter and peace. The valley and mountain top experiences are what makes us who we are. It's the DNA of life. Every sunrise and sunset we witness is a "GOD WINK" at us and a sign that life is good no matter the valley or mountain we're facing. What's thought provoking is, as we transition from one season to the next, what was the lesson(s) learned? Lessons not learned will be repeated.

God winks at us to give us direction in the form of wisdom and knowledge but are we listening and being obedient? God winks are personal experiences that are classified as divine intervention that are perceived as an answer to a prayer.

God winks in the valley. It is written in Psalm 23:4 (AMPC), *"Yes, though I walk through the [deep, sunless] valley of the shadow of death, I will fear or dread no evil, for You are with me; Your rod [to protect] and Your staff [to guide], they comfort me."* When God is a comforter, He brings healing.

God winks on the mountain top. It is written in Isaiah 40:31 (AMPC), *"But those who wait for the Lord [who expect, look for, and hope in Him] shall change and renew their strength and power; they shall lift their wings and mount up [close to God] as eagles [mount up to the sun]; they shall run and not be weary, they shall walk and not faint or become tired."* God winked at me in my deepest valley experiences and as I'm soaring to my mountain top experiences that He has purposely orchestrated for me, I can identify His winks through my journey.

Can you identify when God winks at you giving you wisdom, knowledge and understanding in your darkest moments? When we can recognize God's divine intervention in our life, it brings healing and peace.

Sincerely,
Pamela Grant

<u>Affirmation</u>

I Am obedient to God's voice and attentive to His winks. I Am spreading my wings. I Am soaring with the eagles. I Am moving with power and strength. I Am full of Godly wisdom.

About the Author

Pamela Grant is a servant of Christ, pastor, worshipper, prayer warrior, wife, mother, and grandmother. She loves God, her family and traveling. God has open doors of opportunity to broaden her to have compassion and empathy with an impact on women ages 40-65 and elementary school youth who feel they are "not good enough and don't fit in." Through Pamela's pastoral nurturing, teaching, experiences, discernment, and God's wisdom, she inspires her sphere of influence to have confidence, know they are valuable, are good enough and have purpose. As a leader, she is evolving and committed to growth.

Pamela has an Associate Degree in Business Management, Masters in Theology, Leader School Alumni, certificates in Pastoral Care and Women of Worth & Worship. She is an Inspirational Coach, co-founder of Kingdom Impact Ministry, founder of Kingdom Pearls of Wisdom, God's Purpose Seekers, and founder of Alway Driver Improvement School.

Pamela can be contacted via email at kingdompearlsofwisdom@gmail.com.

Letters Written By Patricia Jackson

My Sister, My Heart

My Dearest Sister,

Your picture is still etched in my mind and heart. I see you standing 5'7", 160 pounds, simply gorgeous, holding your precious baby girl. You loved life. I was livid when your health began to decline, which resulted in your transformation at the age of 23. When you shared your belief of what happened to you, my immediate thought was, you trusted the wrong people. "Poisoned," you said! I almost fainted. I believe that because your symptoms were never diagnosed. Three years later, you transitioned because of pneumonia. Wow! Now, I was left with having to find forgiveness in my heart for those you alleged were responsible for your death.

The love I have for you made it so hard to forgive those whom you believed were responsible. You asked me to forgive them. What made it hard was visualizing how you transform to a 4' fetal position, 80-pound frame laying in that bed, unable to speak or move from where you lay. I knew in my heart that the Lord would repay all those involved. I was not as rooted in Christ as I am now. I wanted to take matters into my own hands but God's Word says, *"Beloved, never avenge yourselves, but leave it to the wrath of God, for it is written, 'Vengeance is mine, I will repay, says the Lord.' To the contrary, 'if your enemy is hungry, feed him; if he is thirsty, give him something to drink; for by so doing you will heap burning coals on his head.' Do not be overcome by evil, but overcome evil with good"* (Roman 12:19-21 ESV).

My flesh was telling me they took away your voice and your life. My heart would break every time I would say I loved you and you could not say it back. I was left with the hope that you were saying it in your heart.

They took you away from your baby girl. It took a moment but Sissy, I have forgiven them, so I write this letter in hope that someone will find it in their heart to forgive someone they believe or know may be responsible for the death of their loved one.

The disciples asked Jesus, "Who is the greatest in the kingdom of heaven?" He replied, "Truly, I say to you, unless you turn and become like children, you will never enter the kingdom of heaven" (Matthew 18:1-3 ESV). I kept my promise and am looking after your baby girl. You also have three grandchildren and one great grandchild you have yet to meet. They all look like you and talk plenty just like you.

Love,
Your Big Sissy

<u>Affirmation</u>

Today, I let go of the anger and resentment and I choose to forgive for my own well-being. I am also choosing to let go of resentment that tries to weigh me down and hinder my growth and happiness.

The Last Twelve Hours

My father suffered a stroke and had to be placed in a nursing facility. He was the seventh and the last of the household to leave me. Daddy was a strong and powerful man in statue. He was a strict disciplinarian in the home, yet so passionate, gentle, and affirming with others outside the home. I felt I was his pride and joy, but he never said it to me. I needed him to verbally validate and affirm me. I needed him to say, I love you or I'm proud of you. Finally, in the last 12 hours I spent with him, he said those words.

Dear Daddy,

Thank you for the last twelve hours you spent with me. They meant more than you'll ever know. I can't imagine how I would feel now had you left without ever having that moment. You left me a memory I can never forget.

Those last twelve hours taught me a valuable lesson. Never take loved ones for granted, time is precious, and cherish conversations and short visits. Saying "talk to you later" or "I'll see you tomorrow" has taken on a new meaning for me.

The last twelve hours with you also helped me to understand the importance of being a good listener. Life is so unpredictable; your stroke impaired your speech and hindered you from ever making another sound. The next

106

day, no one could have told me I would never hear your voice again.

Daddy, I'm so thankful to God for giving us those twelve hours of GRACE. Daddy, I have no regrets about talking to you from 4:00 PM until 4:00 AM. We both needed that. You needed to be forgiven and I needed to hear you will forever love me and I was that daughter that any Daddy would love to have. Wow, there it was, the validation and affirmation I needed to hear. When you said you have bragged about me to your friends and you read every article and watched videos of me, it brought so much closure. Thank you, God.

Love,
Your Beloved Daughter

Affirmation

I am so deserving of love and understanding, regardless of my father's actions. I choose to heal and find love with myself and from others whom God sends into my life. I will also open my heart to any other sources that God provides for me.

He Came for His Wife

Dear Husband,

I write this letter to you because I am so grateful to God for gifting me with a man like you. The odds were stacked against us, and many thought we wouldn't make it because we met and seven months later, we were married. God had a plan!

Our marriage was ordained of God. I didn't even know you, but I was able to witness your first sermon. I was a guest at your first preaching engagement. It was a divine set up. In the Spirit, you were my husband before I said I do. My prayer to God was always a prayer that my husband would love God because I believed if you loved God first, you would love me forever.

It was strange how we met, never dated but became friends first. On your first visit, you fell asleep while sitting on the sofa talking. Suddenly, I heard snoring. You almost messed up God's plan. However, when you woke up, this is what you said with such confidence, and I quote, "I'm not looking for a woman/girlfriend. I came for a wife and she must understand that my love for God is first and foremost."

God will give you your words back, that's my prayer. I was totally shocked, but what an amazing feeling to know God heard me. My husband found me. The Scripture says, *"He who finds a wife finds a good thing and obtains favor with the Lord"* (Proverbs 18:22 ESV). Three months later, we were married.

God is so amazing! Seven months has turned into 29 years and counting. I am so proud of the man you have become. My love for you grows stronger day by day. You are my provider, problem solver, and not to mention putting up with all my unique ways and ideas. I feel I don't say it enough, but I want you and the whole world to know you are truly my king chosen by God. So, my love, please believe your acts of kindness and your love for me is always noted. You are such a passionate man, yet stern and yes, set in your ways; however, I wouldn't trade you for anything or anyone.

Forever love,
Your Wife

<u>Affirmation</u>

My commitment to my marriage is admirable and my love has the power to withstand any challenges that may arise. My marriage is a beautiful partnership built on love, trust and mutual support. Together, we create a lifetime of happiness and fulfillment.

Everything the Enemy Wants
You to Believe is a Lie

Dear Sister,

As you read this letter, I want you to know I'm praying for you. I may never know your name, but God does. I know you in the Spirit and know I love you, my sister. Blood does not make us family but in the Spirit, I am the sister who's fighting for you. I'm a firm believer that I am not my sister's keeper, but I am your sister and I'm praying for you. I pray that every lie the enemy has told you be destroyed in the name of Jesus. The enemy wants you to abandon your opportunity to be the woman God has called you to be and that is a lie from the pit of hell.

Someone or you yourself only believes you're just a wife, mother, sister, caregiver, someone's sounding board, or even someone's punching bag. Perhaps you have been made to live in silence. I stand in agreement that you embrace who and what God has called you to be. In spirit, I see you sitting, asking, "Why you?" You talk to yourself saying, "This is not the path I had envisioned for myself."

I want to encourage you to hold on. It's not too late. Greatness still awaits you. You have not missed your opportunity. 1 Corinthians 2:9 (ESV) says, *"What no eye has seen, nor ears heard, nor the heart of man imagined, what God has prepared for those who love him."* It is not too late. You will be who God has called you to be. Just believe.

I hear you doubting, Sis. I see you. Where do you begin? Start by knowing you are valuable. Know your self-worth. For your worth is more priceless than rubies. I love you, my sister. Don't let anyone tell you who you are. Know who you are and have confidence within your heart. Turn your pain into prosperity and your tragedy into triumph.

Your Sister in Christ,
Patricia Jackson

Affirmation

I am capable of finding new paths and rediscovering my passion. I will make a choice to embrace my inner strength and trust God in all things. I deserve happiness and fulfillment in my life. I release all doubt and fear that's trying to hold me back and I surrender myself totally to the will of God and not others.

I Believe in Prophecy

To the Reader of This Letter:

We're living in a season where the Lord has put a word in the mouth of the prophet for the Nation. Ephesians 4:11 reads *"And he gave some, apostles; and some,* **prophets***; and some, evangelists; and some, pastors and teachers;"* The ministry gift of the prophet, as we understand it, is a prediction or forecasting of future events that bears witness to what we, in some instances, already know. The gift of a prophet shows up in various forms—in dreams, visions, or direct messages. Other times, the Lord may use a prophet to provide guidance or give warnings or insight to those who are present.

Prophecies of guidance and direction on many occasions to an individual(s) are so necessary. God will send the prophet to minister in places where people need clearer instruction or conformation to the word they have already received from Him. Sometimes, you may know you hear from God, but you pray for clarity, not doubting, but just confirmation to pursue the opportunity to be sure you're in alignment with the purpose and will of God for your life.

Thank God for the men and women who bring correction through prophecy. It is hard when God uses someone to speak correction, but I think of it as the solvently and God showing His love to keep us in alignment by protecting us from danger or bringing harm to ourselves. Our willingness to change once we receive the instruction also shows that we love and trust God with His plan for our lives.

God gave me this prophecy for 2023. In October 2022, the Lord said to tell His children in this season He's going to move expediently, He is going to expedite the blessing that have been held up by the enemy and we will receive expansion in the year of 2023, and He will bless everything our hands touch for the next seven years. Receive the word of the Lord in Jesus' name.

From Patricia Jackson

Affirmation

I trust in the wisdom of God, and I am open to receive guidance and insight through prophecy. I have faith; therefore, I believe in the power of prophecy to provide clarity and guidance for my destiny.

About the Author

Patricia Jackson is a Licensed and Ordained Pastor, Author, Conference Host, Motivational Speaker, Transformational Coach, Entrepreneur, and business owner with over 30 years of ministry and marketing experience.

Patricia is the Co-Founder of St. Jude Worship Center Church, Former Satellite Administrator of Truth Bible Institute (Theological Seminary, ORU Tulsa, OK), Founder of United Women for Christ Ministry, Founder of Bible Truth Live Broadcast, and the Founder and Director of Community Care Outreach Center 501(c)3 Non-Profit Organization.

Married for over 27 years to Pastor Russell Jackson, blessed with a host of children and grandchildren. Patricia has dedicated her career to helping others be healed, set free and delivered through the word of God.

Author Contact:

https://linktr.ee/pastorpatriciajackson

Instagram: bibletruth_copastorjackson

Letters Written By
Dr. G. Landry

Trusting in God

Dear Reader,

I hope this letter finds you in good health and high spirits. I wanted to take a moment to share an incredible story of hope and transformation, a testimony to the amazing ways in which God can turn around situations that seem utterly hopeless.

Recently, a young lady came to me with a seemingly insurmountable challenge. She was in a period of deep despair and uncertainty, where the world around her seemed to crumble, and all her hopes and dreams were on the verge of collapse. The circumstances were overwhelming, and she felt utterly powerless to change them. It was during this time that she experienced a profound encounter with God, a moment that would forever transforms her perspective.

In the depth of her distress, she turned to prayer, seeking solace and guidance from a high-power God. She

poured out her heart, surrendering her fears, doubts and burdens to God, acknowledging her limited understanding of the situation. In that moment of vulnerability, she felt a sense of peace wash over her, a glimmer of hope amid the darkness.

Days turned into weeks, and as she continued to trust in God's faithfulness, she witnessed a series of events that defied all odds. Doors that had long been shut suddenly swung open, presenting opportunities she could have never anticipated. Relationships that were strained began to heal, and support came from unexpected sources. With each passing day, it became increasingly clear that God was orchestrating a miraculous turnaround.

The journey was not without its challenges. There were setbacks, moments of doubt, and times when it seemed easier to give up. However, every time she was tempted to lose heart, she reminded herself of God's unwavering promise to never forsake her. In those moments, she held onto her faith with renewed determination, believing that God's timing is perfect and that He works all things together for the good of those who love Him.

Slowly but surely, the situation began to transform before her eyes. What once appeared hopeless and irreparable was now filled with possibilities and a renewed sense of purpose. As she reflected on this incredible turnaround, she was reminded of the profound truth that God's power is limitless, and His love for us knows no bounds.

Through this experience, she has learned invaluable lessons about patience, trust, and surrendering control. She witnessed firsthand the power of prayer and the incredible ways in which God can work in our lives when we place our faith in Him. It is a testament to His unending grace and mercy, and she is forever grateful for His intervention.

I shared this story with you, not to boast or elevate myself, but to offer a glimmer of hope to anyone who may be going through a seemingly hopeless situation. Our circumstances do not define us, and even in the darkest of times, there is always the possibility of a divine turnaround.

May you find solace and strength in this testimony, and may it remind you that God is always with you, even when the road ahead seems treacherous. Hold on to your faith, lean on God's promises, and trust that He is working behind the scenes to bring about a miraculous transformation in your own life.

In His Service,
Dr. G. Landry

<u>Affirmation</u>

I am called to be that certain Samaritan to care and help others where I can. I am letting my love matter to others today.

Life Lessons as a Woman in Ministry

Dear Woman of God,

I hope this letter finds you well. As a woman who has dedicated herself to ministry, I wanted to take a moment to share some of the valuable life lessons I have learned along this remarkable journey.

It is my sincerest hope that these insights will encourage, inspire, and guide other women who are called to serve in ministry. When I first started in 1970, they were not allowing women to get near their pulpits. And don't even think about coming into their church with pants on and no stockings. Simply out of the question.

They forgot that Jesus entrusted us with more than they realized. He blessed me today to see just how far things have come. Allow me to share ten life lessons for you as a mighty woman of God in ministry. We've come a long way, baby!

1. EMBRACE Your Unique Calling: Each one of us is fearfully and wonderfully made, with distinct gifts and talents. Embrace your unique calling and recognize that your role in ministry is invaluable. Trust that God has specifically equipped you for the task at hand, and your voice and perspective are essential in advancing His Kingdom.

2. NURTURE Your Spiritual Life: Ministry can be demanding, often requiring us to pour out our hearts and souls for others. However, it is crucial to prioritize your own spiritual well-being. Make time for prayer, study, and personal reflection. Allow yourself to be filled before pouring out to others, for you cannot give what you don't have.

3. SEEK Mentorship and Community: Surround yourself with wise mentors, both male and female, who can offer guidance, support, and accountability. Seek out fellow women in ministry to form authentic connections and cultivate a sense of community. Together, you can navigate the unique challenges and celebrate the joys that come with serving in this role.

4. EMBRACE Your Strengths and Weaknesses: Understand that you do not need to be perfect. Embrace your strengths and use them to uplift and empower those around you. Recognize your weaknesses and be willing to seek help and support when needed. Vulnerability is not a sign of weakness but rather a strength that fosters trust and authentic relationships.

5. DEVELOP Healthy Boundaries: Ministry often blurs the lines between personal and professional life. It is essential to establish and maintain healthy relationships and boundaries to prevent burnout and maintain healthy self-care, rest, and recreation.

Taking care of yourself allows you to better serve others.

6. EMBRACE Diversity and Inclusivity: The body of Christ is diverse, encompassing people from various backgrounds, cultures, and experiences. Embrace this diversity and seek to create an inclusive and welcoming environment within your ministry. Be intentional about amplifying marginalized voices and addressing social injustices, working towards unity and equality.

7. LEARN From Failure and Setbacks: Ministry is not without its challenges and disappointments. Embrace failure as an opportunity for growth and learning. Recognize that setbacks do not define you but rather refine you. Trust in God's sovereignty and allow Him to turn your trials into testimonies.

8. PRIORITIZE Continuous Learning: Commit yourself to a lifelong pursuit of knowledge and growth. Stay updated with theological advancements, engage in professional development opportunities, and seek ongoing education. Cultivate a humble and teachable spirit, always willing to learn from others and expand your understanding of God's Word.

9. PRACTICE Self-Reflection and Evaluation: Regularly evaluate your motives, actions, and goals in ministry. Engage in self-reflection to ensure that you are aligned with God's purpose and that your ministry is bearing fruit. Seek feedback from trusted

individuals to gain valuable insights and make necessary adjustments.

10. CULTIVATE a Heart of Love and Compassion: Ultimately, ministry is about loving God and loving people. Cultivate a heart of love and compassion for those you serve. Let your actions be rooted in empathy, grace, and kindness. Remember that you are a chosen vessel of God.

Ministry just isn't about looking cute and being in control. It's about being obedient to the Voice of God and following His directions.

Go with God,
Dr. G. Landry

Grief Hurts

Dear Reader,

I am writing to you today with a heavy heart to share the deep grief I have been experiencing since the untimely passing of our dear friends Officer Robertson, Yolanda, Donna, and Lucille, who succumbed to the devastating effects of COVID-19. I find relief in writing this letter, knowing that you understand the profound impact these friends and team members had on our lives and the huge void absence has left behind.

The news of their passing was a total shock with one being right behind the other. It reverberated through our office, team members, and through our circle of friends, leaving us grappling with an overwhelming sense of loss and sadness. They were all not just a friend but each a pillar of support, a confidant, and a source of constant joy in our lives. Their infectious laughter, warm smile, and genuine kindness were a beacon of light during even the darkest times.

As we reminisce about the moments we shared with them, we are flooded with bittersweet memories. From our carefree adventures helping others and late-night conversations to countless celebrations and comforting embraces during times of sorrow, they were all there, radiating positivity and love. Their ability to bring people together and create a sense of belonging was truly remarkable, and their absence has left an indescribable void in our lives.

The circumstances surrounding their passing make it even more difficult to process our grief. The cruel and relentless nature of COVID-19 has robbed us of the chance to say a proper goodbye, hold each other close, and to find solace in one another's presence. The pain we feel is magnified by the knowledge that we were unable to be there for our beloved friends in their decisive moments. It is an immeasurable loss, and we are left grappling with a mix of emotions that range from anger and sadness to profound gratitude for the time we had together.

In the midst of this grief, I find comfort in the memories we shared and the lessons they taught us. Their passing serves as a stark reminder of the fragility of life and the importance of cherishing every moment we have with our loved ones and friends. It compels us to hold our dear friends and family closer, to express our love and appreciation more frequently, and to make the most of each passing day.

As we navigate through this difficult period of mourning, I want to extend my heartfelt gratitude to you for being there for me and for sharing our collective grief. Your presence and support have been invaluable, and I find relief in knowing that we can lean on one another during these trying times. Together, we can honor all our friends and family memories by carrying their love, compassion, and zest for life within us.

While the pain of losing them will never completely fade, I am hopeful that with time, we will find healing and strength. We will strive to celebrate their lives, their accomplishments, and the mark they left on each of us. We will hold dear the memories we created together and find solace in the knowledge that their spirits will live on in our hearts forever.

Please know that I am here for you, and I hope we can find comfort and support in one another as we navigate the waves of grief. Together, we can honor all of their legacies and find the courage to face the future, carrying their light within us.

With deepest sympathy and love,
Dr. G. Landry

Affirmation

I am letting my love matter to others today.

About the Author

Dr. G. Landry is a well-known community activist, national and international speaker, teacher, author, ordained minister of the Gospel, and highly sought-after authority on the topic of homelessness and non-profit community programs. She is affectionately called Mom G by the hurting in her community, city, state, and across the nation.

She is the founder of several programs which include Helpers for the Homeless and Hungry (The Original HHH), Women's Network for Cancer Prevention of which was founded in 1970, Caregiversspeaks.org, Magi's Blessings Children Ministry, Women's Prison Ministry, and Catch The Vision TV Ministry Landry's Daughters-Landry's Son's A DAY OF LOVE AND LAUGHTER.

Since 1970, she has been helping thousands in and outside of the United States to include London England, Africa, St. Croix, St. Thomas, Belize, and Haiti. Her main emphasis being on reaching the lost at any cost.

Contact Dr. Landry for Speaking and Training Sessions at Drg5639@gmail.com.

Letters Written By
Mei Mak

Letter to Mother

Dear Mother,

Where do I start? It has been a long journey of life without you. However, I would like you to know that I have invited God into my life in my early twenties, and through His unfailing love and strength, it has given me hope to walk this road called Life without you being by my side.

I now have become a mother of teenage children. I know and understand the love and hard work that you did for our family.

During my younger years as a teenage girl, the years without you were the toughest. I wished you were around, so I could feel your love, hugs and support, and ask you many questions about life.

Mother, I just wanted to thank you for your big and unconditional love you had shown my siblings and me. I wish I could do more to help you during your last days in

the hospital bed—resting and getting through each day with pains.

Now that I am an adult and a mom, I know what pain looks like, and the challenges I face are difficult at times as well.

I have so much good news to tell you, from different employment and the various ministries I have the chance to participate in, to meeting my husband who is now the dad of our children. I also have the opportunity to serve God globally and walk out my faith in Christ Jesus. The list of blessings just goes on and on.

All these experiences have shaped the person that I am today. That will be another letter to write to you, Mom.

I hope and pray you are at peace and live in a place where there are no more pains and sufferings. I am sending you my deep love, appreciation and big hugs. I just wish you were here to see and enjoy the blessings that God has bestowed onto my young family and me. I also wish that I could bring you out to a beautiful dinner to celebrate you on this Mother's Day!

Mom, I just wanted to say, "I love you" and wish you were here with us.

Lots of love,
Your daughter, Mei

Affirmation

I am blessed. I am stronger. I am wiser. I am kinder towards myself. I am grateful for all that I have in life. I am resilient. I am God's masterpiece. I am who God says I am. I am a child of God.

Letter to Young Mei

Dear Young Mei,

How are you today? Maybe you are wondering why you are receiving this letter…I've got the chance to write this as an adult to you. It is not easy, but I will try.

First of all, I want you to know that you are a special child of God. At some point in your life, you will encounter God and it is a road He has paved for you to travel. The road will not be easy, so be prepared to face challenges, but also to enjoy life's beautiful moments.

Always have an open mind and reminder not to judge yourself or anyone. You have a heart of love for your family, friends and even strangers. That is who you are, and it is also a gift from God.

As you travel along life's path, beware of the toxic people you will come to work with, as well as the difficult managers you have in your careers. Though this sounds tough, it will get better as time passes and with God's grace you will learn to forgive them. You will have many people who can see how hard you have worked and they will try to help you out in return.

New opportunities will come your way, so do look forward into the future.

All the bad times you were going through will also strengthen you, and that is when you will stay closer to God and seek His strength and guidance.

You have many caring and supportive friends who are always there to cheer you on and to encourage you to shine!

So, after all, life is not as bad as it seems. Writing to you as an adult, I also tried to stay positive and trust in our God for daily strength, hope and peace.

His love and grace is never ending. The Bible says, *"...he will never leave you nor forsake you"* (Deuteronomy 31:6 NIV). It always gives you hope reading it.

Another thing I will share with you is, during midlife, you will do great things and achieve your ambition. So, be encouraged and stay strong because many people need you, and they are inspired by your actions, love and kindness.

One more thing, I would like to remind you to believe in yourself, and do set boundaries early on in life, so you can stand firm and be true to yourself. Not to please others, but to please yourself and honor God.

Until next time, do take care of yourself, your health and enjoy life's beautiful moments.

With love and prayers,
Your older self, Mei

Affirmation

"Be strong and courageous. Do not be afraid or terrified because of them, for the LORD your God goes with you; he will never leave you nor forsake you" (Deuteronomy 31:6 NIV). This verse in the Bible has always been encouraging to me and I hope you will find it helpful too.

Letter to Heavenly Father

Dear Heavenly Father,

Thank You for Your love, Your peace and Your grace. Thank You for yesterday, today and tomorrow. Thank You for perseverance, strength, wisdom, compassion, joy, forgiveness, and the will You have given me.

Your Word has encouraged me to stand up, stand firm and to move forward every day, even though some days are harder than other days. I have learned to lean on your Word and to show up to do what I need to do—to walk out my faith and continue my ambition to share Your Word with others.

I thank You, dear God, for the amazing sisters and brothers in Christ who have been a wonderful support to me. I am grateful for them and for all Your blessings. Your love is so deep, wide and vast. Your grace is beyond our understanding, so thank You, Lord Jesus, for being with me, my family and my friends each day. May I continue to serve faithfully and be a channel of Your love, to share and to bless others and in turn they will pass on this great love of Yours to their family and friends. It will be a beautiful ripple effect.

I pray for those who are seeking You right now. Lord, please soften their hearts and bless them with hope. Wherever they are Lord, and if they are going through tough times that others don't seem to know or

understand them, You will understand them God. Please watch over them and guide them to a safe place and please send them help.

For those of us who may be walking with You for a long time and do not have a support group to help them stay active in their faith, I pray You will direct their path and bless them with good and caring Christian friends. Renew their love for You, God.

Thank You, Lord, for being my personal Savior whom I can call my Heavenly Father. I am blessed and I am loved. In Jesus' mighty name I pray, Amen!

Your child,
Mei

Affirmation

"I can do all things through Christ who strengthens me" (Philippians 4:13 NKJV). I hope this verse will be your prayer also. God bless you!

Letter to First Time Moms

Dear Friend,

Congratulations to you and your husband as you celebrate the birth of your first child. The labor pains are over and what a great relief to be able to hold your newborn baby in your loving arms.

I can remember those special moments. I will be open and frank to share with you that being a first time mom or dad will not be easy. I wish there was a class where we could learn "how to be a mom and dad" in a classroom, but then again, it will not be a "one size fits all" scenario because each child is different and unique, just as God has created us to be.

At times, there will be many sleepless nights, fatigue and feelings of loneliness. I hope and pray you will have a good support system in place to ensure that you take good care for yourself and your spouse. Reach out to family members, friends or even hire a babysitter who can assist you both so you can nurture each other as well. It is good to communicate openly and honestly with your partner if things seem to get out of hand.

Remember to set some time for yourself and have time out with your friends so you can be yourself again. Being a young mom is hard work and challenging when you are on your own with no one to talk to or to help you out. I remember crying out to God for help when things became overwhelming and there was no one around. He gave me strength to carry on. Motherhood happened to be a bigger task than I expected!

The love of being a mother doesn't end; you will soon forget about the labor pain and plan for your second baby. The reward is great and what you learn about being a parent is priceless. It teaches you grace, love and forgiveness; as well as how to be a better parent and a better person.

It carries an immense responsibility with the blessings of joy and laughter. Treasure the beautiful bond you have with your children and look back on the progress you have made as a family.

May God always bless you with joy, love and the energy you need for the wonderful mom that you are. Keep smiling, be kind to yourself and love yourself more. Put your faith in God, pray and trust Him for your future.

You are a great Mom!

Love and big hugs,
Mei

Affirmation

When you feel exhausted, you may like to read this verse. I am empowered by God's grace. *"Come to me, all you who are weary and burdened, and I will give you rest. Take my yoke upon you and learn from me, for I am gentle and humble in heart, and you will find rest for your souls. For my yoke is easy and my burden is light"* (Matthew 11:28-30 NIV).

To Those Who are Stigmatized

To Those Who are Stigmatized,

This is a letter for you. Whether you have an illness or are different from your peers, do not lose heart because there is hope. Don't give in to their comments because you are a strong, special and unique individual. I will mainly be focusing on our health.

There are many situations that one might be stigmatized upon. Here are some examples: Having an illness or a disability, not knowing a new language in a new country and being discriminated from work; also your body shape, race or mental health. There is no shame in having an illness or if you are not good at math or science. When I share about my hepatitis, people tend to generalize and stigmatize my illness. These comments show the ignorance of others.

Therefore, whatever your situation might be, there is no shame; for you do not choose to be where you are. People do not know you and they judge you. The main thing you need to do is to first love yourself, to stand firm in your own right—seek and pursue help for your health, find the right guidance so you will not go through this alone.

Keep going, keep trying—for there is hope! You will get over this. Try saying this: "I can do all things through Christ who gives me strength," a verse taken from the Bible, Book of Philippians 4:13, which has been a help to

me. Be grateful for today. There is hope for your situation and God hears you, just call out to Him.

I wish you strength, hope and love. Keep your head up high and be proud of who you are. You are valuable and you are loved.

God bless you always,
Mei

Affirmation

I am no longer allowing anyone to define or label me based on my size, hips, lips, or fingertips. I am loving on me.

About the Author

 Mei Mak is an Entrepreneur, a Speaker, a Certified Personal Stylist, and a Moderator of Bible Reading Audio 365. She is passionate in helping people and also an Advocate for Hepatitis B, which she has written many talks on.

She is co-authoring an anthology with Dr. Carolyn Coleman, together with fifteen amazing women of God, titled *We Write the Letters That Heal*, which is her first book.

Mei Mak lives in Australia with a Chinese background. She is a devoted wife and mother. Being a Stylist, she loves helping women look beautiful. She is an Ambassador for God and her Christ centered life is the essence of her letters. She can be contacted via email at styledbymei22@gmail.com.

Letters Written By
Lana M. McQuinn

From Brokenhearted to Restored

Dear Reader,

It's 12:23 a.m., dreadfully beyond my bedtime. Yet, I'm wide-eyed, my body is limp and my mind is racing with visions of life's scenarios dancing in my head. There are no signs of rest. Nonetheless, I can feel the peace of God. Eyes squinting, glasses just out of reach, searching for a glance of the time once again, I hear a comforting melody whispering in the distance. *"Raised out of the ashes, I'm singing and dancing. You put me back together. I am fully accepted, always welcomed here, because you love broken people."* It is at this moment when I recognize how He's preparing me for what's to come.

The song God used to minister to my soul in that moment is entitled *Broken People*, written by Israel Houghton. I laughed. Isn't it funny how God has a timely and peculiar means of capturing the attention of His children?

I grabbed my journal from bedside, scrambling upon

a fine point pen. Finally, I began to write just as instructed by God. But first, He led me to the Book of Romans and then to Galatians. Unsure of the significance of where He was taking me, I knew I was being led by Him.

The same message He shared with me, I pray yields comfort to you. I had been led to the books of Romans and Galatians as a reinforcing lesson on Paul's challenge to remain steadfast, unmovable, and totally reliant on his faith in Christ. The old saints would say it this way, "You got to hold on!" After losing my uncle, grandmother, brother, grandfather, and the man I thought I loved, I needed reassurance that God was with me. Nights were lonely and tears could have produced glaciers. The fortitude to hold on was excruciating, but I held on relying on hope to lead me to healing and restoration. I can imagine that the expulsion from Rome left Paul brokenhearted, yet he persisted in challenging both Jewish and Gentile Christians to unite in peace. Paul urged the Romans to live not "according to the flesh," but rather by the spirit (Romans 8:30).

Let's not forget how Paul's later days contradicted his previous lifestyle. He is even noted as being radical in his beliefs and character. He was not always revered as a Saint. He was humbled by God. Can't we all relate? At one point, I had totally lost myself. I tried to emulate that which everyone demanded of me. Like Paul, I made so many mistakes that I'm not proud of, but I had to spiritually mature and seek God's purpose for my life. It took losing people I have learned to love even more as a result of death, false friendships, and even failed relationships to inspire my next level of spiritual solitude. Conviction and adoration activated a determination to seek, pray and cry-out so my soul would not be lost. Now, I can testify that God mended my broken heart, restored my faith, and has provided purpose with increased provision. He can do the same for you.

Wow, what a transformation I have become. I'm grateful for all the trials and tribulations. I am happier than ever because of the people God sent into my life to push me to greater potential. I'm grateful. Never again will I doubt myself. Paul's message insists that redemption, sanctification, and regeneration is found in our faith in Christ. Don't allow the world to convince you of insanity because they don't understand your spiritual gifts and relationship to and with God.

Paul's influence and message to the church remains relevant today, just as it was over 2,000 years ago, and just as it were that restless night as God ministered to me through song and scripture.

Be encouraged and remain focused as Romans 8:31 declares, "If God is for us, who is against us?"

Sincerely,
Lana McQuinn

Affirmation

This is the season of rest, restoration and renewal. Grab a hold to it and seek your purpose in Him. To God be the glory, Hallelujah.

A Letter to My Daughter Zsnita

Dear Zsnita,

When I first saw you, you were the joy, the sweet bundle any mother could want in a daughter. Your smile lit up the room. Oh, don't forget those beautiful bright eyes. Hmm, so gorgeous. I thank God for you.

You've grown to be such a beautiful, wonderful young lady, a mother, and a wife. Yet still, you keep pressing and pressing each day. It's marvelous to see how you've developed from that little baby doll into a mature woman.

I thank you our long talks. I thank you for the tears we've cried and the conversations we've had. You give so much joy and so much love. Always remember Psalm 30:5, *"weeping may endure for a night, but joy cometh in the morning."* Continue to walk in your joy. I thank you for being my anchor and source of strength.

As you continue to press forward, rely on Proverbs 3:9 to be your guiding light, *"Honour the Lord with thy substance, and with the firstfruits of all thine increase."* Keep pressing on, my dear. Keep striving, praying and hoping to receive the good things God has in store for you. Dare to continue to dream high trusting in God to guide you each step of the way.

My love for you will never end. You're the second heartbeat of my life. Oh, let me change that, you're the third heartbeat of my life. And I love you so. In rainy

141

weather and stormy seas, remind yourself to seek the face of God and know that He will hide you beneath His feathery wings. Rise and walk, in Jesus' Name. The sky is the limit for you.

Love,
Your Mother

<u>Affirmation</u>

Always tell your children how much you love them.

My Second Heartbeat, Michael

Dear Michael,

Where do I begin? I was blessed with you, my son. My first bundle of joy with big chubby cheeks and a huge smile. When I first saw you, you brought tears to my eyes because I couldn't even fathom that I was going to be a mother for the first time. To see you walk, crawl, cry, it was so overwhelming. To watch you grow was amazing. Umm, and look at you now. I cannot call you my little man anymore, but you know I still do.

You're successful, married with four children, and still trying to tell me, "Mom, I need to try to keep me straight." What can I say? Thank you. Not only are you my son, you are also my best friend. When things are tough and I don't quite understand what's going on, you tell me, "Mom, don't worry." When you got older, you just kept saying, "It's ok, Mom. It's all good." You kept me smiling. Of course, you always said, "Mom, you shouldn't do this. You shouldn't do that."

When you were younger, I told you that you're not grown until you accomplish this, this, this, and this. And when you turned 18 and graduated, what did you say to me? "Mom, I'm grown now. I'm not that little boy anymore. I'm grown now."

I'm so proud of who you became and who you are becoming. I thank God for your life. I thank God for the wisdom that He's instilled in you. And I know even when things were getting tough, when you used to have your moments, you would call and say, "Mom, what are you doing?" When I said nothing, the next thing I knew, within an hour, you were knocking at the door in the middle of the night saying, "Mama, I just had to come see you." I used to love when popped up like that.

I've always taught you to be independent. There are some things I wish I had never taught you to do because now that I'm older, you're doing it. But I thank God for that. So, I want you to know, yes, you're my second heartbeat because God gave me my own heart first. And I love you. I love you so. You're always going to be my baby boy. I don't care how grown you get.

Keep praying. Keep striving. Keep going for those dreams you have. Don't let anybody take your peace away from you. Keep being the man God has called you to be. From this heart to your heart, I love you.

Love,
Mom

<u>Affirmation</u>

Your children are a gift from God.

144

To My Father

Dear Heavenly Father,

Before I say anything, I ask for forgiveness, Lord. For You already knew my path when You created me. You knew the wrong things I was going to do, the wrong things I was going to say, and how I was going to act. So, Father, I ask for forgiveness.

I could never thank You enough for the life You have given me. As a child, I always felt alone, like I was the only one. Even though people and family were around, I always felt alone. But one thing I can say is you gave me solace. I could talk to You and take a walk with You. I remember those things. And even though people kept telling me I was crazy, I was seeing things, I was saying the wrong things, I thank You, Lord, for allowing me never to forget those things. I knew I was loved and I still fell in love even though I did not love myself.

I had a complex life. People mistreated me and did and said things to hurt me. I never thought I was good enough for anything or anyone for that matter, not even myself. I'm so grateful You allowed me never to think of suicide, Father. Thank You.

I thank You for my family who I grew up with, Lord. My grandparents and my mother took us to church and taught us morals and values. I thank You for that.

I thank You for the people who I thought were my friends growing up. They really weren't, but I thank You for them anyways.

I thank You for all my trials and tribulations, and my loneliness. I thank You for those nights I cried.

Father, thank You for my children. Thank You for all the gifts that you've given me, Lord. I thank You for my mother and my siblings. Lord, I thank You for the people you've brought into my life who have come to help push me along the way for Your will, to do Your will!

Lord, I thank You that before my grandmother passed, she said one thing to me, and it still sticks. She said, "Lana, you need to go back to your first love. I see you've been talking to God." I didn't even know my grandmother knew. I didn't know what she knew. But I thank You because those words were what I needed. I ask for Your forgiveness because I was angry, and I left You so many times when You didn't leave me.

And thank You for bringing my brother who I always knew I had into my life. I thank You for him and his wife and children. I also thank You for all my uncles. But most importantly, Lord, I thank You for the people who are in my life now. I've lost a lot of people I thought were friends along the way, but I had to realize that not everybody's a root. I guess that's why you kept giving me that sermon on Ecclesiastes 3. Everything happens at a time and season. It hasn't been an easy road but I'm getting there, and I thank You.

I thank You for every one of those whom You allowed to speak into my life for Your edification. My life has changed. I thank You for allowing me to see.

Even though I felt I didn't have a place, I thank You for allowing me to now be the David for my family. Father, there's no words to express how grateful and thankful I am. And I ask in the name of Jesus, Father, please continue to cover me. Help me to walk this straight path. I want people to see You and me and not me and my frailties.

I thank You for growth. I thank You for understanding. I thank You for the wisdom that You're giving me. But most importantly, Lord, I thank You for Your Son Christ Jesus who died to even allow me to live. Thank You. Thank You. This is my prayer to You.

In Jesus' Name, Amen.

Affirmation

Give God the glory each and every day.

About the Author

Lana M. McQuinn is a minister, professional senior consultant, business owner, co-author, mother of two children and grandmother of seven. She has a Diploma in Computer Information Systems, Associates in Theology, and Bachelors in Christian Education. She can be reached at lm.mcquinn@gmail.com.

Letters Written By
Elizabeth Miller

Unlashing the Mute Button to Heal

Dear Reader,

I grew up in a household of thirteen people with two parents, two grandparents, one great grandmother, and eight children. Being the baby of the eight, you can trust and believe I was not spoiled.

I always felt like I was muted throughout my existence. From trauma to being bullied in school to hurtful relationships to me hurting others to feeling like someone was holding my mouth down with their bare hands over my mouth, I felt trapped inside my body trying to be free. Whenever I did say anything, people around me always told me to hush and be quiet, they said I didn't have a say in the matter or I was too old for that, etc. It started to shut me down as a woman and, as a human being, it made me frown. Therefore, I began to not say anything at all. When I went out to eat and my order was not right, I just ate it and didn't say anything

about my food thinking it would be all right. Then about six or seven years ago, I broke the mute button of my life.

God spoke to me one day and things started to change. He said, "Break free, My daughter, you have something to say." My healing process had slowly begun to take place unlashing that mute button of my life. Right there, I started to weep in my Spirit all the way down to my feet. He gave me Psalm 147:3, *"He heals the brokenhearted and binds up their wounds."* I began to read His Words and that was what sought me through. He said, "Use My Word, My daughter, to heal your broken wounds. I catch every tear you drop, so hold your head up and let your voice speak out. You are the queen I made you to be. Stand proud, stand tall because you are representing Me." So, whatever may hold you back, step forward and release your mute button. God's got your back.

Grace to you,
Elizabeth Miller

Affirmation

I am strong. I will not be muted any longer. I will take the muted button and cast it out to the sea. I am free to be. I will walk with the ability to take control of the mute button because God is in control.

A Seed of Healing

Dear Lord,

I'm a seed in the ground. My healing is dark under this ground. I asked, "God, can You pull me up from the ground?" You said, "Not yet, daughter. You have not spouted. Just look around." So, I live in this dirt in the ground.

How can I start this healing process under this ground? Let me think and pray and seek Your face every day. First, thinking of all the good soil You brought me through. Digging deep in Your Word so I can be true.

Lord, I pray one day You will get me out of this dirt but until then, I will make it all the way to the church. I love reading Your Words so let me be still. I want to listen to Your voice. It brings me chills. God, I'm ready to receive a good Word from You to bring me out of this dirt of healing so I can push through.

You spoke again saying, "It looks like you gained a root from within. But you still must go through the process so your life can begin to heal." So, I said to myself, "What is making me feel like I'm not growing enough?" Yes, I have one root but why, God, am I still in this dirt and feeling so much hurt. I want to see the sunshine even on a cloudy day. Please help me, God, to have a breakthrough. Can there be any other way?

I think I must forgive myself and others too. Oh God, rest upon me and pour Your holy oil into my soil. Break

151

me free so that I can be free indeed. I'm ready, God. Come back to me. You spoke back and said, "You are already free. Just walk in the newness of life. You have come out of the dirt that's the amazing life."

Thank you, God, for loving me so. You are so amazing, don't You know.

In Jesus' Name, Amen

Affirmation

I will take root in knowing the soil. I'm the seed that will grow strong. I will shake the dirt off my feet and move on to greater things that God has for me. I will not crack in my faith.

A Letter to My Daughters
with a Healing Heart

Dear Daughters,

I sit here thinking about the relationship we had and I'm having that feeling of I wasn't a good parent, or in other words, I could have been there more for you. People have expressed what a good job I have done with my children, but once again, I feel I could have done more. As a mother, I didn't receive instruction on how to raise my children or even have a blueprint. All I had was what I knew growing up, but I still felt like something was missing.

A few years ago, we found ourselves learning more about each other. You stayed mostly with my parents and my grandparents until they went to be with the Lord. I have worked basically all my life and am still doing so now. I worked to provide a stability life for you and make sure you were good in all areas. Plus, with all the hustle and bustle of everyday life, I never really knew you and you didn't know me.

You always saw that strong mom, conquering the world. But behind closed doors, I was broken inside and I needed to heal. I love seeing your friends interact with their moms/parents and the closeness that they share. I can admit I was a little bit envious because I didn't have that relationship with you. But when God showed up more in my life and I learned how to stop beating myself up and love myself for just who I am, the healing started to flow. Once I gave it over to Him, the seed from the root began healing.

Now you and I have a beautiful relationship and we are evolving each day as God gives us breath in our bodies. Just know God can turn things around once you surrender to Him and be obedient to His Spirit. We, as parents, must find that resting place to heal. God will do the rest. Just sit back and be still.

Love,
Your Mother

Affirmation

I will love my daughters with everything in me. I am a strong positive mom. I will show and strategize my daughters to know their worth. I will show them they can be the best they ever can be.

I Believe in Love

Dear Reader,

Believe in love. You must know it is yours all over again.

Believe in love as you connect the dots of your heart in the shape of knowing that you have destined what only God can unlock.

Believe in love for the real love, the unconditional love, and maybe true love.

Believe in love. He or she is out there believing just like you. So, don't feel down, just look as new.

Believe in love and be true to yourself. Stop looking for a man or woman to validate the rest.

Believe in love. You know what you want. Seek God first before you mess it up.

Believe in love. Don' t be sad or blue. The Father sent His only begotten Son. That's the amazing love that is true.

Believe in love. Forgiveness is true. Don't hold back. Release that hurt so you can feel fresh like the morning dew.

I believe I will love again someday, but I had to get over the hurt that I have held so long that God could not make away. So, now I'm open and deserve the love I desire that God wants me to have. But I am on a mission for God. He will make filter so I can grow through and stand. I have purpose to fulfill for God, the faith in the field beyond the stars.

You have purpose too. Hold your head up and keep pushing through. God knows what is best for you. Stop looking at that man or women to bring you out of your shell so you can be brand new. God is a healer through all your pain. Stop and think, He created you with a twinkle in His eyes from the stars above. Trust in Him in all your ways, even on cloudy days. God said it is yours in the making. Write it down and make it plain. He will give you that man or woman because He reigns.

Blessing on you,
Elizabeth Miller

Affirmation

I deserve the love. I'm worthy to love again. I'm open to love. I want to love. I will not look for love in all the wrong places. I will let God lead and guide me in love. I will have an open mind.

Healing of Not Being Forgotten

Dear Reader,

I am a child of the King, oh yes, that is me. He hasn't forgotten, oh that I may see. As the daybreak comes on the ocean sea, oh how I remember He hasn't forgotten about me. When I look into the sky, I get all choked up inside. I know God hasn't forgotten about me. When I speak with power and authority, He turns it around for my good. I know He hasn't forgotten about me for sure. I know my Lord hasn't forgotten about me even when I have the dark night. His Word states in Isaiah 49:15-16 that He will never fail you or forsake you. He will walk with you through every dark valley. I will continue to let Him lead me by His own mighty hand. Lord, use me with your healing hands. By His grace and mercy, I just want to understand. I know He hasn't forgotten the master plan.

I know that I can rejoice because I have a voice. No man or women can shut me down. I wear His crown. He knows my name with Jesus' sound, oh I exclaim. He says continue to be free in me because I AM the great I AM and that is all you need. He hasn't forgotten about me; He will make my pathway straight. I just have to trust Him and open the gate. He hasn't forgotten about me.

I feel God healing me from the inside out. I feel His love that surrounds me, I can shout. I know He hasn't forgotten about me. I will share with the world so they too can glee.

God has not forgotten about you. Keep striving for bigger and the best you, no matter what people say. Look into God's eyes way up in the clouds and see how white they are with such pureness they even know how to bow. Be real with God and be true to you. He will find you in the field of faith that is so true.

Blessings on you,
Elizabeth Miller

Affirmation

I have not forgotten. I will not be forgotten in God's eyes; He sees and knows all. I know it will be all right. I will stand on what I know, be proud and stand tall in whom I know. I will confess with my own mouth to shout with praise with no doubt.

About the Author

Elizabeth Miller is known for being a purpose pusher. She is a mother and grandmother. One of her personal quotes is by Shakespeare, "To Thine Own Self Be True." She became aware of herself by finding her voice, recognizing she matters, and knowing she is enough. She is always looking for opportunities for growth as a woman of God. Her passion is to push people into their purpose, those who want more out of life to be great in what God instilled in them to do. While on her journey, she is a deacon, lyrical dancer, and teacher. She has studied and earned Certificates in Leader Theory, People Theory, and an Associate Degree in Christian Counseling. She loves spending time with God and getting to know Him better as God downloads into her so she can make an impact on family, friends and the community in which she lives. Contact her on Facebook, Instagram, or email faithnthefield@gmail.com.

Letters Written By Dr. Linda Roberson

When Help Turns Into Hurt

Dear Helpful,

Have you ever experienced church hurt? Many times, I have opened my heart to help people. The end results range from great to horrific. The impact can build someone up or break them down. People with compassionate hearts can be vulnerable. I was. Even praying about matters, we must move forward with God's wisdom, listen to Him, and guard our hearts. King Solomon reminds us in Proverbs 4:23 (NIV), *"Above all else, guard your heart, for everything you do flows from it."*

Unfortunately, we can be taken advantage of by people, but when it is church hurt, it hurts at a different level. God knows everything and will still bless us. I've made some crippling decisions in my life and ministry. They taught me that some hurts only God can heal. We all go through painful experiences. I have been used, lied to, stolen from, suffered financially, and had credit ruined

160

all during one of the most critical periods in my life. What led to it? Simply answering the call for help.

One experience involved a pastor and church that I knew very well. They needed funding for their building project. Upon being asked, and after praying about it, I helped them by obtaining the funding. The burden of guaranteed repayment rested on me with their guaranteed commitment to pay it in full. I was to be financially rewarded. Things went smoothly for a while and then plummeted downhill like a rolling boulder. It was horrific and I never received one red cent or one brown penny of compensation. I suffered much pain with domino affects; severe collateral damage that hit hard mentally, physically, spiritually, emotionally, and financially.

Spiritually, I was bleeding and on life support, yet I continued to serve faithfully in ministry. For years, I suffered in silence and beat myself up over and over again. With tears streaming down from my eyes I would ask, "Lord, why me? All I was trying to do was help." God doesn't forget our labors of love.

I continued to question and seek God, openly confessing that I was severely wounded. He was the only one who could heal me. Even in the midst of what I was going through, God did some incredible things for me. He taught me the power and necessity of forgiveness, the kind that goes much deeper than the surface. We're talking about diving into the core of the heart, beyond pain, emotions, self-pity, and everything buried within. I could never articulate the depth of the hurt, but God knew how bad it was. Also understand that the enemy would like nothing more than for us to stay attached to pain. Christ heals and makes us free and teaches us the importance of forgiveness. On the Cross He prayed, "Father forgive them for they do not know what they do" (Luke 23:34 NKJV). My healing started when I began to forgive, and I relied on the Holy Spirit to teach me how to do it. I also had to pray for the others and myself. It wasn't easy. Since then, God has given me beauty for ashes, joy to replace mourning and a praise garment to replace the spirit of heaviness. I had to move on because God has greater and better things in store. He healed me in my silence so that others could hear my voice of recovery and be healed. No matter who you are or how you've been hurt, God can heal you and use you to help others. Even as I write to you, He's still healing me.

Let go of the pain. It will hinder your progress, growth and blessings. I know it hurts; I didn't go through my experiences just for me. It was for you, and others, to be healed and made free. I pray that you will trust God and ask Him to bring you out of that place of hurting. Know that He can and will heal you, remove the pain and make you whole. Ask Him and believe.

Your Sister in Christ,
Dr. Linda Roberson

Affirmation

I am better because of what I went through. God is healing me to write my story. I am completely healed, made whole, and free. Now I'm walking into the greater that God has for me.

Unbound from the Box

"Therefore if the Son makes you free, you shall be free indeed" (John 8:36 NKJV).

Why am I stuck here?
It seems no one cares
I'm engulfed in self-pity,
Opportunities, accept them I don't dare.

Why am I constantly crying?
Pacifying the deep wounds of hurt
When God has so much more for me
My mindset is blocked, not alert.

I can't worry about the past
So, I've been overlooked,
Talked about, and mistreated
So was Jesus, I read it in the Book.

The pain is so real
My wounds bleeding deep
Even my spirit hurts
Suffering in silence; I didn't breathe a peep.

Hurt in the Church,
Hurt in the world,
Hurt in the family,
Hurt by your own self, Girl.

And I sat there alone
Rehearsing all the scenes
Like a movie set in my mind
Take one, two, and three.

It drew me deeper and deeper
Into a treacherous abyss,
Extremely dark and submerged
Where I didn't need to exist.

Listen, it's past time!
Get up off the ground!
I had been wallowing and rotting
In that box I carried around.

I thought no one saw
Or that no one even knew
Now, the Heavenly Father has sent me
To breathe life back into you.

Know now who you are
God gave you your name,
Not what people call you,
"My Child" is His claim.

You're the apple of His eye
He made you to be free
Not bound by people or circumstances
I speak healing to you and liberty.

Be healed from every hurt

Inflicted by the wounds of man
From every word spoken against you
And everything not in God's plan.

Wholeness to your spirit
Every place filled that is void
Sound mind, renewed, and transformed
Everything detached that had you annoyed.

Get out of the box!
Bust wide open if you must
Remove the limits and pressure
Remember, it is in God that you live and trust.

The only box to entrap us
Is the one that we create
Today, stand free in your liberty
Never return to the box you escaped.

Affirmation

I am free and released from the things that had me bound. I walk daily in Christ's liberty where no box or limits can be found.

You Have a Heritage

"Behold, children are a heritage from the LORD, The fruit of the womb is a reward" (Psalm 127:3 NKJV).

To the Childless Woman:

Do you want children? I did. They are a blessing from God. Please be kind to yourself if you have tried and not yet succeeded. We don't always understand the "why" in our lives. I know the depth of that desire. I've been there. I have also seen God turn situations around. He is faithful and trustworthy.

I started serving God at an early age and loved learning about Him. Though I was young, I knew I wanted four children and a family after marriage. As I became older, I focused on my career and education, and put the career over my personal life desires. I was consumed with working and adopted tag lines like "I'm too busy" or "I don't have time." Later, I got engaged, but the relationship ended. Why am I sharing this? Because I want to encourage you. It's easy to stay focused on what we want, but we must also be open and not miss what God is trying to give.

As the years progressed, I continued praying and believing for children because that was my desire. I said, "God, You know I want children." At first, I wanted four, then three, then two, and then one. I can remember humorously asking God, "Can You give me a half?" God

understood and the laughter brought healing to my heavy heart.

My most painful awakening was the day I turned the big 40. I looked back over my life, thinking about the dreams that had not come true. My heart felt crushed. Two friends came over to help me celebrate my birthday. It reminded me of Job, though my experience was nothing compared to his. They tried to encourage me, but I just listened. No one knew the depth of my desire or the pain I felt. But I still trusted God, knowing that He had a plan for me and He would reveal it in time.

I read about women in the Bible who wanted children. At this point, I had served the Lord for many years and was committed to Him. He blessed me with nieces, nephews and godchildren and I was grateful. I thought about God's promise to Abraham of his heir through Sarah. Both of them laughed at different times because they were old and she was barren. They tried to make it happen in a different way. But as God promised, she became pregnant and gave birth. God had the plan and promise for them, and us too.

The older I got, the more at peace I became. I realized that just because a woman doesn't give natural birth doesn't mean they are not a mother. God spoke to me one day. I had transitioned to a new church to serve in ministry. He said that the people I serve will become my children. I honestly didn't know all of what He meant, but I knew it was my promise from God. The more I served, built relationships, taught the Word, and loved them, the more the revelation became revealed. Many were spiritual children, more than I could ever birth, and I nurtured them. I have people older than me calling me Mother. The relationships are based on love, just like God's relationship with us.

There is an abundance of people, at all ages, that need love, hope and spiritual guidance. I'm grateful that He chose me and gave me that desire of my heart. He blesses us with opportunities to impact people's lives and help them to be all that He purposed them to be. They are our heritage.

So, to the women who desire to have children, God has no limits. He can truly do exceedingly and abundantly far more than we can ever ask for or imagine. Don't give up on your dreams and desires. God knows you and sees your heart. Keep it open to Him. He has not forgotten about you.

From Dr. Linda Roberson

Affirmation

I am confident that God will intentionally bless me, according to His plan, and at His appointed time. I am trusting God, daily walking by faith and accepting His will.

I am confident that God will give me the desires of my heart. I am encouraged and will help those who need my love and guidance. I open my heart to accept God's will and plans for my life.

About the Author

Dr. Linda Roberson is the founder and CEO of Live In Purpose which provides counseling and coaching to individuals who are stuck in life and held captive by the past. She is known as the "Live in the Now Coach."

Dr. Linda Roberson received her PhD in Christian Counseling from DCCJ/Kingdom Theological Seminary, holds a M.A. in Divinity and a B.S. in Business Administration. She is also a certified Leadership and Life Coach.

With a compassion for people, Dr. Linda Roberson passionately teaches individuals how to be healed from past issues and hurts, live in the now and create a better tomorrow. Her ministry expands over thirty years. She has been featured on The PIC TV Network. She fulfills her purpose through using her gifts and talents to equip, encourage, and build others.

Dr. Linda Roberson can be contacted at www.Liptoday.com.

Letters Written By
Apostle Rose Ann Thomas

Hidden Secret of Silence

Dear Curse Breaker,

This missive awakens hidden emotional baggage that crippled and almost broke me in the early stages of my adult life. I had built up anger and penned up childhood trauma whose walls and closed doors had to be opened if I wanted to be free of what I now know were generational curses. As I put pen to paper, floodgates of childhood trauma and abuse surfaced like a volcano. My childhood's hidden, unspoken, and silent abuse was now speaking. The windows of my memory bank now screamed **enough** to set me free.

What had been suppressed memories awakened identifying its role and names. Other family members went through the doors, unable or afraid to identify the root cause of spousal and alcohol abuse, teen pregnancy, and incest to name a few. The "what goes on in this house stays in the house" scenarios had given silent permission for the abuse to continue unaddressed. Journaling has been the navigator which allowed me to identify and dismantle the triggers of abuse that held me hostage for most of my adult life.

Hidden beneath the surface of the bitterness, hatred, unforgiveness, and anger deep in the file cabinet of my heart was unspoken pain for unspeakable acts stemming from childhood. I watched our neighbor's son take little kids into his room after his mother left the house. He must have been thirty years old, and I was five, but God kept and protected me. Living with fear inside, having nightmares, afraid to sleep in the dark. My aunt could not understand why I didn't want to go next door. I couldn't tell her of the threats. I now recognize that fear kept me bound and made me an accessory to abuse by my silence.

As a child, I was not equipped with the mindset to know how to speak up and call out the bad acts of adults. I know it made me feel fearful and not safe. The fear of being the next child to be molested consumed me. Can you imagine carrying the guilt of others' pains so young? I had anger and silence inside of me. I moved back home with my parents, but the memories lingered. Silence is a dark place and living in fear will destroy your self-esteem. I challenge parents to never tell their children to do whatever an adult tells them to do. I know the intent is to teach children to respect adults, but some adults are not entitled to respect.

The challenge is to teach our children to communicate any and all feelings that cause fear to enter their spirits

immediately to their parents or care providers. Keep the door of communication open with your child and stay on guard.

Mothers, be alert and on guard to who watches your child. Be that overprotective mother. Yes, teenage pregnancy was a part of my life event, drinking, gambling, and dropping out of school. It was not until I had the most extraordinary experience with God that changed my life. The Holy Spirit light overshadowed and there was an outbreak in me. Washing and healing all hurts. Cloves of fire were on my tongue. I began to thank God for what I was feeling in my spirit.

I learned how to do spiritual warfare. I learned the power of my tongue and how to use it to destroy the enemy's plans. I began to pull down strongholds in my family; "no more curses." It is over.

I recognized that the Holy Spirit was within me. All my daughters finished high school, and I finished high school and received an Associate Degree in Theology.

My message is to encourage you to come out of the closet of your pain. Free yourself and identify the triggers that have depleted you of your womanhood and love of self. It is the time to stop and give yourself permission to address the past and graduate from the pain. Protect your children and teach them how to discern right from wrong and to speak up whenever they feel uncomfortable or afraid of any adults regardless of their station in life.

Sincerely,
Apostle Rose Ann Thomas

Affirmation

I am a daughter of the Kingdom of God who will never be afraid of abuses, rejection spirits, or negative words of man or woman again because I am stronger in the Power of God now! I move in the I am strength. Greater is He that is in me.

All things are possible to them who believe. I am a believer of the Word of God. For He is the lifter of my head. Therefore, I give thanks for everything that comes into my life.

From Tragedy to Triumph

Dear Reader,

Have you ever needed health insurance and not had it at a time when you needed it the most? I lost health insurance in 2013, so I couldn't get mammograms regularly. In December 2015, I had a mammogram and was told they needed to do a biopsy. In January 2016, I faced the most difficult season of my life. I was informed by my doctor that I had stage 2 breast cancer. The doctor asked me strings of questions including, "How do you feel after the news you just heard? Do you feel like hurting yourself? Are you suicidal? Are you angry with yourself?" All I could say was, "I love me."

Fear gripped me in that moment. The Holy Spirit reminded me of what Paul said to Timothy, that God had not given me the spirit of fear but of power, love, and a sound mind (2 Timothy 1:7). I made a decision that I would not allow fear to dictate my faith though I had moments when I questioned why God allowed cancer to attack my body.

I was angry and I felt like God had punished me for some act of disobedience. I asked God, "How and why did this happen to me?" I pleaded my case, "I am Your child, God. I am saved and I carry Your D.N.A. I am a D.S.W., a Demon Slaying Woman, and an Apostle over churches."

I have been in ministries for over 50 years. I knew what God could do. I prayed and saw God heal cancer, dry up lumps, and heal face and hand cancer. I have testified of miracle after miracle. I only heard, can you still tell God yes, when it's your time? I prayed and used the anointed oil God gave the ingredients to make. He taught me what to eat and drink to bring healing to my body. The cancer was now at stage 3. After surgery, I underwent Chemo and radiation therapy consecutively for 30 days. Many ask, "Are you in remission?" My answer is, "I am healed." Not only did I survive, but I am also an overcomer. God's miraculous power took me from tragedy to triumph. God is good.

Regards,
Apostle Rose Ann Thomas

Affirmation

I am healed to dream dreams and visions that will sail to the plans of God. I will trust in my maker, for He knows the plans that He has for me. Sky is the limit to my dreams, so I will dream big.

Lord, I Need a Miracle

Dear Parents with Sick Children,

One Friday morning, I heard the helicopter flying over my head but did not know why. I went to work and had no idea my son was being arrested. No mother wants to feel the pain of her child in trouble. I received a telephone call from the police station to say that Kenney was picked up today and charged with armed robbery.

I called my oldest son and told him to go and check on his brother. I always told my children I would not go to jail if they got in trouble.

The night before my son went to court, while I was praying, I heard the Spirit of the Lord say, "What are you going to do when all the odds are against you?" I fell back against the wall and slid down on the floor. I said, "Lord, I need a miracle but I'm going to praise You." He put me in the Book of Habakkuk 3:17-19.

I cried because my 17-year-old son was sentenced to ten years in prison for a crime he did not commit because he failed to turn his friends in. That inflicted more pain.

The day my son got his sentence, I was downstairs praying for another mother whose child was set free. I went home and closed the door to my room shutting everybody out. I had a revival scheduled that night and started to cancel it, but the Lord reminded me of my promise to praise Him. The devil said, "Cancel the service. You are hurting. You can't go before people.

You're the pastor and couldn't keep your son out of prison." My secretary said, "Pastor, the Lord told me to tell you that He spared your son's life. He had to be locked up because they're going to kill him." All I could say was, "Lord, I thank You." During the revival, God saved three young men.

A mother feels pain seeing her child under stress and there is nothing she can do but pray. My eyes filled with tears as I reflected over my life and saw the hand of God over my family. God will heal a mother's pains. My son is now working and starting his own business.

Have you ever felt helpless and knew if God didn't intervene the situation was hopeless? That's what I was facing in May of 2010. My oldest daughter Nikki was hospitalized and was on life support. Prior to the hospitalization, she was not feeling well and running a slight fever during Bible Study. The next day, she went to the hospital to see her doctor. After several hours of not hearing from her, I checked in with my daughter, Angela, to see if she knew Nikki's whereabouts. She said, "Mama, Nikki never left the hospital. She is on life support in the Intensive Care Unit."

My heart skipped a beat as I began praying and calling on the Name of Jesus. I gathered my purse, oil, and turpentine and rushed to the car. The heartbeat of a mother is her children. To know my child was fighting for her life, not able to breathe on her own, left me speechless and heartbroken.

Nikki had two deadly poisons traveling through her

body. When I walked in, I could see tubes everywhere. I laid on my child and said, "Lord, I need a miracle." I cried out to God, "I stand again with a need? Another child is in trouble."

I pulled out my oil and turpentine when Angela said, "They will put you out of this room smelling like turpentine!"

I said, "It will break the fever." I laid on her again, with my hand in her hand and my face on her face, and quoted Isaiah 53:5, "…and by His stripes, we are healed."

By the end of the visit, the fever had broken. That Friday, she started breathing on her own. God showed up in the room. Sunday evening, church members went to the hospital and prayed the prayer of faith over her. Tuesday, Nikki was out of I.C.U. in a private room. On Saturday, she came home.

Put your trust in Jesus and do not lean to your understanding. Always acknowledge God and He will direct your path. Know that God is a healer.

Blessing on you and yours,
Apostle Rose Ann Thomas

Affirmation

I am designed by God. I am blessed and wonderfully made. I am an ambassador for Christ. I am a prayer warrior in the Kingdom of God pulling down strongholds. I am a D.S.W. (Demon Slaying Woman) of God.

Plead Your Case Before God

Dear Friend in Need of a Miracle,

Let me tell you about my firstborn, Cedric. He tried to solve his problems with alcohol. He got so drunk that he passed out on the floor. His drinking buddies left him thinking he would sleep it off. I almost lost my son that night from an alcohol overdose. My daughter-in-law found him and called 911. He was rushed by ambulance to Keener Hospital. He coded twice on the way.

The Bible teaches us to plead our case before God. *"Come now and let us reason together, says the Lord; though your sins are like scarlet, they shall be as white as snow;…"* (Isaiah 1:18 ESV).

"I, even I, am he who blots out your transgressions for my own sake, and I will not remember your sins. Put me in remembrance; let us argue together; state forth your case, that you may be proved right" (Isaiah 43:25-26 ESV).

They were pumping the alcohol poison out of his system. I laid on my son and prayed for him like I had prayed years earlier for my oldest daughter. Yes, I pleaded my case before God and asked Him to bless and save my son. I stated my case and contended with God. I said, "Lord, it's me again. I need a miracle for my son. You did it for me before. I ask You to do it for me again."

My son's alcohol level was 485. The doctor said, "Only one out of ten survive." I said, "He will be one of the ten." With the urging of the Holy Spirit, I began

calling for reinforcement from men and women in the Gospel known to be able to bombard Heaven with effectual prayers. I anointed my son with oil and believed in faith for a miracle. At 4:30 a.m., my son started moving around and by 8:30 that morning, he was breathing independently.

When you are in trouble or in need of a miracle, plead your case before God. Call on those who pray in faith to believe in you. Anoint your loved ones with oil and thank Him in advance for the miracle.

In 2020, Angela, my second child, had headaches every day constantly. When a child is in pain, the mother feels the pain. The doctor found out she had a brain tumor. My statement, "Lord, I need a miracle." I asked, "Are you scared?" She said, "Yes, but I know the scripture. God has not given me the spirit of fear but power, love, and sound mind." I sat on her head as God instructed me on the day of surgery. The word was you're going down in Jesus and coming up in Jesus. The wait got long. The doctor said, "She is good; I could only get 95%. She was going into distress, so we pulled out." Thank you, not paralyzed. I said, "God will heal the 5%." My daughter is walking, talking, driving, and cooking. That was my prayer, Lord, I need a miracle. God did it.

Blessing on you and yours,
Apostle Rose Ann Thomas

Affirmation

I am a mother who knows the power of prayer. Prayers are strong for everybody but made for a praying mother. That's me, that's who I am, a praying mother. A warrior who never stops. Prayer and faith go together like a mother and her child.

About the Author

 Apostle Rose Ann Thomas is the Founder and Overseer of Christ Liberty Family Life Center Inc. of Atlanta, GA. She is the Apostle of New Envision Faith Tabernacle Inc. of Camilla, GA. She has her Certificate as Teacher Aide, Nursing Assistant, Psychiatric Aide, Office Assistant and bookkeeping, Notary, CDA, and Infant and Toddlers Teacher. Her Associate Degree in Theology from the DCCJ Branch of Kingdom Theological Seminary in Jackson, MS. She is also pursuing her Doctorate Degree in Counseling.

She is a devoted wife, mother, grandmother, preacher, teacher, and chaplain. She loves her family and church. She is a Harriet Tubman in her own rights and has been an opening door to many. She is a marriage counselor and a spiritual advisor with the knowledge of God.

D.S.W. (Demon Slaying Woman) of God. Saying: "Preach Apostle, I believe I will!" Motto: Christ is first and the center of my focus.

She can be contacted at Rathomas1061@att.net or Rathomas1061@gmail.com.

Letters Written By Penelope Tiam-Fook

Who Am I Becoming?

Dear Reader,

I once read a quote by Brian Tracy that said, "Change your thinking and you will change your life," and I genuinely believe what he said. When I was a little girl, I remember running around the yard without shoes on. Climbing trees, picking fruit right off the branches and fruit juice dripping through my fingers with each delicious bite. Life was good and the memories priceless.

Fast forward to watching my daughter run around the yard barefooted filled me with joy until a new lot was being cleared near my home. Deer began to pass through my yard frequently. And soon after, the tick bites I experienced resulted in my health declining rapidly along with the diagnosis of Lyme Disease.

I believe there comes a point in our lives when we are faced with choices that determine what the next path of our lives will look like. I had a choice to make. I was angry

184

about the deer passing through my yard every day; about the barefoot moments being taken away from my daughter and me. Angry that I now had Lyme Disease. Yet, choosing anger would keep me stuck in the past.

I soon realized that I didn't want to live with anger. It was time for us to break up. It was time to change my focus and my thinking in order to change my health.

Choosing to regain my health put my focus in front of me instead of looking back. And in so doing, I wrote the words below to keep my focus forward throughout my healing journey:

> If I want to be happy, I will wake up with purpose. When I wake up, I will be curious about what I can do today. I will seek to find the good in my day. Even in the midst of pain and discomfort, I will choose joy. I will choose love for it heals any and everything in me. I will choose to love who I am becoming at the start of every day.

Grace be to you,
Penelope Tiam-Fook

Affirmation

I am enough and I choose to be in loving harmony with my body, mind, and soul.

My Joy Is Wonder-Full

Below every layer of pain
Inside every muscle of weakness
Between every crevice of inflammation
Within every layer of unwellness
Every layer of disease
Exists my truth.

I am joy.
Overjoyed with an abyss of great delight.
I am sacred.
Devoted and dedicated to demystify the false nature of
    illness surrounding me.
I am reverent.
I hold deep respect for my true nature.
Woman. Daughter. Sister. Mother.
Kind. Compassionate and Authentic.
I am a divine light of love everlasting.
My joy is abundantly wonder-full.

I am thankful for this moment.
I am thankful for the sacred gift of life.
I am thankful for every breath of life flowing within me.
I am thankful to be able to access joy at anytime,
    anywhere.
Joy is my faithful companion and always with me.
Joy and I are one.

Affirmation

I am grateful for all that I am, for my joy and wonder and all that is.

Love is the Way

Living day in and day out feeling unwell sucks.
My soul whispers to me, "This is not the way."
"Then what is the way," I ask.

Love!
Life's Only Valuable Emotion.
Life's greatest energy in motion.

I want to be filled with abundant, peaceful, joyful love!
Love that has no convincing or persuading.
Love that feels so divine, so exquisite, so connected
That word spoken to my soul, into my being
Touches deep within the secret chambers of my heart.

Love is like the key that unlocks mystical treasures.
My heart and every cell in my body will know its song.
The frequency of its vibration,
Each note and melody resonating deep within me.

My mind will recognize the tune.
My soul will hum in harmony.
My body will sway hearing its sweet melody.
Nothing forced. Love is light, healing and free.

<u>Affirmation</u>

Love is healing every part of my mind, body, and soul
today and every day.

188

You are Beautifully
and Wonderfully Made

Dear Reader,

There are good days and bad days. Today was a stressful day! Some days will be like that, feel like that. Some nights won't offer much sleep and the mornings that follow will sometimes start with the thought that nothing will go right.

Sometimes, caretaking feels like an unrewarding job. And some days, it seems like no matter my effort, the negativity I encounter feels like I'm being drenched by a waterfall filled with the noise of dissonance.

In those moments, it is harder to honor who I am. Kind, considerate, compassionate. It's hard to shake the dissonance, to remember how amazing I am when I'm absorbing the negativity of those around me.

Yet, in these moments, my courage rises up to remind me that I am better than the ungratefulness, the negativity, the stress. I am beautifully and wonderfully made by my Creator.

I am more than these low vibrations. I may feel broken down in this moment, yet I am more than this moment. The light in me sees and honors my true nature and my Creator. Therefore, I choose to rest and reset my energy, my mind, and my thoughts. And when the sun shines upon the horizon, I will rise for I am beautifully and wonderfully made.

Sincerely,
Penelope Tiam-Fook

<u>Affirmation</u>

I am beautifully and wonderfully made and my soul knows this very well. This I believe!

My Teachers are Yes and No

Am I strong enough to walk away from whatever or whomever

Are not aligned with my values, my energy, my way of being?

I was brought up to be respectful to my elders, to be pleasant and obedient.

Yet, in culture that expects women to be reserved and hold their tongues,

A girl can unknowingly be conditioned into people pleasing behavior.

I was brought up to pursue the American dream.

To go to school, get a college degree, get a good job, start a family.

Yet, there isn't a whole lot of educating in school about the stress that comes with

Pursuing the dream. Or the silent speak that weaves the false web around you

Creating a new, yet subtle definition about your self worth.

Or the performance goals that dangle approval with recognition or promotion for a job well done.

There isn't a whole lot of education about work-life harmony.

Yet, the reality is that there is a lot of power in saying yes and saying no.

Yes gives others the power to utilize my wisdom for their greater good.

No gives me the power to utilize my energy for my greater good.

No is teaching me to let go of people who are not aligned with who I am and want to be.

No is teaching me to let go of any negative energy I am holding onto within me.

Yes is teaching me to let in people who inspire and uplift me and who themselves are growing too.

Yes is teaching me to enjoy rest, having a good time and to see the good in others.

Yes and no, my teachers, have given me the power to know when to let go and when to let in.

My health depends on making these bold, courageous choices.

Affirmation

Letting go is a process. As I let go of past hurts, wounds, and relationships, I feel good, really good! I choose to honor, love, and respect myself. I have the power within me to decide what I want and how I want to live my life.

About the Author

 Penelope Tiam-Fook is a Spiritual Well-Being Coach and Functional Nutrition Consultant, and founder and owner of TIAM Wellness, a women's functional nutrition, wellness and soul-care practice that empowers women in leadership to transform persistent stress, burnout, and fears associated with a health diagnosis to reclaim their hope, health and wild woman soul. She offers women the opportunity to set soul-affirming intentions and engage in the practice of spiritual kintsugi to unmask the woman the world wants them to be to remember who they truly are. Connect with Penelope on Instagram @TiamWellness.

Letters Written By
Shalonda "Treasure" Williams-Lynard

The Liberty that Comes
From a Father's Acknowledgement

Dear Rev. Daddy,

First, let me say that I miss you. It almost seems strange to say that because I do not feel like I was around you enough to miss you. Yet, I do. Maybe it's the dreams of having time with you that I miss. My mind travels back to my fourteenth birthday. I got so upset because it took you so long to say, "Happy Birthday." The anger that I felt came from a place of hurt because I wanted and needed your attention.

Fast forwarding to my birthday in 2019, this time I find myself sitting next to you in your hospice bed. With discernment, much prayer, and an inner understanding of myself, I came to understand a new truth. Things were as they were supposed to be. God is intentional and He knew what was best for me.

It was through my experiences that I learned how to depend on and trust in God. I now conclude it was not His will for you to raise me. Yet, I know now that you understood me.

After watching you sleep for a while, I tapped you ever so gently on your shoulder and whispered, "Daddy, it is my birthday." As weak as you were, you looked at me and gave me the biggest, brightest smile that I had ever seen grace your now 79-year-old face. I will forever treasure the words that flowed from your lips. Though time had taken hold of your voice, though weak and faint you said ever so proudly, "Happy Birthday Daddy's Baby." I felt sweet liberty.

At age twenty-one, I felt like I had crossed the red sea of forgiveness. But it was at the age of thirty-eight I knew total healing had taken place between you and me. The healing was complete.

Three days later, you crossed over.

So, I started this letter by saying I miss you, but I really wrote this letter to simply say, "Thank you, Rev. Daddy, for participating in my liberty."

I love you always,
Shalonda Yvonne a.k.a Daddy's Baby

Affirmation

I am purposed to be alive, and all things are working together, beautifully, for my good. I was created on purpose, with purpose, to live out my purpose.

Sisterhood is Not Defined By DNA

Dear Val,

Sissy, when I got the news of your crossing over, I felt as if I had been punched in my gut, and the rivers of my eyelid overflood endlessly. Putting pen to paper to announce your passing left me void and perplexed. It was difficult and a little troubling because I felt the need to explain who you were to me.

I named my siblings; you were in that number and I did not feel like the "foster" part mattered. So, why suddenly did I feel the need to explain it to anybody? Why the nudge to share this distinguishing fact now? It was after writing the post that I understood sisterhood in fullness.

Sisterhood is not defined by being blood-related only. It went far beyond bloodline and family. It was woven with true love and friendship and a deep commitment to trust and share our hearts. Too often, limited beliefs make people believe that sistership must be aligned with bloodline. When I think about our talks over the years, I understand better what you were attempting to relay. You were grateful for whatever anyone did for you. You, my sister, just wanted to be understood and accepted as is. I realized that I understood you better than you knew. We shared that common thread.

Many people search their entire lives looking for a sense of belonging amongst their kin. Their thirst to be

valued by the people they shared DNA with and to be acknowledged by family is justified. Who wants to feel the need to perform to feel loved?

I have always known I was loved by my biological family. It was the people outside of my bloodline that I wanted to accept me. That is why I loved you so very much. I wanted you to know that you were my sister and blood was not the defining reason.

It is my prayer that you crossed over feeling that. Thank you for treating me kindly, Val.

Writing that post revealed what a blessing it was to have you in my life. People who are kind and loving are a true gift to mankind. And you were one of them. A gift indeed.

I will love you always,
Your Sissy, Shalonda "Treasure" Williams-Lynard

Affirmation

I am always surrounded by love and as a product of that love I will, in turn, give it in overflowing measures daily. As long as I live, out of my heart will flow love, especially for those who have lived so long without experiencing it.

Stanka

Dear Mr. Tee,

2016 was the year that changed my life forever. It was the year that I lost you and up until that time, I had never felt a loss that deep. God had given me great peace through those three weeks, but in that moment, I felt like all the air had left my lungs. It happened suddenly. I was standing there when they walked in, and I even remember speaking to them. Then they lifted you with that sheet and blood started flowing from your mouth. My chest began to cave in and I remember feeling very lightheaded. It was a good thing that Aunt Pam and someone else were there to catch me and sit me down before I hit the floor. In that short moment, I felt all the tears that must have been hiding away come flooding out. It felt more real than the moment they announced your heart had taken its last flutter. It hurt so badly.

Honestly, I believe I must have felt our time together ending in the physical indeed. No more praying needed, it was over. I started feeling all the things that we had endured together, your struggles and mine. I watched you go from alcoholic to sober. You caught me being a fast tail girl in your living room. You know, those type of things. Yet, all in all, our closeness remained. You loved me as if I was from your very own loins. It would make you very upset when people would say to you, "Oh man Tee, why didn't you tell me that Shalonda wasn't your 'real' daughter?" That used to eat you up, Daddy! I would always say, "If he wanted anyone to know, he would have told them." But in all of the 35 years you were in my life, even after you and mama divorced, I was still your Stanka. And I will always wear that name proudly. I will also always be grateful for the three weeks I was able to care for you before your passing. It was not even a good portion of all you've done to take care of me.

Love & Thanks Always,
Your Stanka

<u>Affirmation</u>

I am greatly valued because God saw fit to create me. I am His wonderfully made daughter, and I will forever stand confidently in this truth.

Rest Sweety

Dear Rebecca,

Sister, I still am not sure if I have adequate words to express how I feel about your leaving. I want to think about it from a positive, glorious perspective, but that is difficult, even after three years. See, your presence in my life was one I could never take lightly.

Because there were so many years between us as siblings, I felt cheated out of time to not only be your sister, but your friend. Once I became an adult and we could actually hang out, it was so dope! I would happily anticipate our talks and trips because I knew they would be absolutely amazing. Honey, we laughed so hard, cried so vulnerably, and prayed so deeply. Me, you, and Coco would get together and just cut up. Oh, how I miss you, Becky.

There are some things I will always hold onto though. Things that actually ring in my heart and spirit very often. Maybe even the top three memories from our span of time together. One would be when we took the road trip down to bury our father. It was all we could do to keep our emotions in check, but we did it! We held each other up by singing, joking, and stopping to take pictures and collect memories. Your sneaky tale was always taking sleep pictures. Well, good thing I was cute and no slobber was caught on film. Lol!

200

Another one would be the night we traveled together to see our brother, whom neither of us had seen in over 30 years. We all took turns singing songs of love. It was the night you sang the song that I would later sing over your body. And guess what, Becky? You still are my sunshine!

The third one would be you being there to help me get ready for my first wedding. Though the marriage didn't last, the vision of you with a huge, proud look on your face as you snapped pictures of your baby sister, will forever be etched in my heart and mind.

Continue to rest sweetly in the arms of I AM,
Your baby sister loves you.

Affirmation

I am full of memories that remind me of how beautiful life is. Life is worth living. Love is worth giving. Faith is worth activating. God is simply divine in all He has created for us to enjoy. I am living life to the fullest.

Letter to My Inner Child

Dear Shalonda,

Obviously, I am not writing because I am grieving the physical death of you. That won't be happening for quite a while according to a few words that you've received. "With long life you will be satisfied," is what they've said. I received that. Yet, I still write this letter because I can feel your grief bubbling over.

You have lost much, and you have been taught over the years not to dwell too much as one who does not have hope. But the losses at this present time still matter. They may seem trivial to those who have yet to endure them. They may appear minute to the one who has determined to never allow others to see them vulnerable. But, my dear self, you are not them. So, I encourage you to feel it all and give yourself grace to do so.

The loss of your fathers, sisters and grandparents play a part in the heaviness of the grief, but you cannot pretend the divorce didn't leave you feeling like you'd lost pieces of yourself. You shouldn't act like the children reaching adult ages and leaving home one after the other doesn't squeeze your heart. Please don't skip over the grief you feel as God continues showing the "all truth" of life and spirituality that you've been asking to see. The tearing down and/or shifting of anything that you've held as valuable can leave you feeling a sadness that many may never understand. And that's ok, Shalonda. You know

that it is ok to admit you're not ok, as long as you hold on to the tools you have to get back up again.

Remember this, you were created with those emotions, so it's ok to experience them. Never let anyone tell you otherwise. But know that I believe in you and the work that you have left to do. So, feel it, cry about it, scream if you need to, talk to wise counsel when necessary, and lie still in the arms of God manifested in the love of your life. Then, take a deep breath, smile genuinely, and thank God you're covered under His shadow. You are safe.

I love you,
Love Self Always

Affirmation

I give myself the same grace to grieve that I would give a friend. I allow myself to feel my sincere emotions because they matter. I am honest about where I am at all times. I am absolutely sure that I will overcome, so I choose to keep all masks off so I can breathe God in and live.

About the Author

Shalonda Williams-Lynard is known to the world as The Nspirational Treasure. She is the appointed Apostle, Prophet & visionary of Love Walk Outreach Global, where she lives to spread the message of The Great I Am spoken and displayed through Yeshua the Christ, that closer walking starts with love. Shalonda is a Certified Life Coach of over 13 years, award-winning inspirational speaker, CEO, media personality and influencer, poet, and best-selling and award-winning author who has written and collaborated on 21 books to date. She lives with an inspired cap of purpose to impact the lives of women everywhere with love and transformational empowerment that reminds them that they are loved unconditionally by God, more than enough for their purpose, and worth all the amazing things that they are desiring. Her ultimate message is this: "Let's heal your soul, so you can be free in your spirit."

Acknowledgements

<u>Dr. Carolyn Coleman</u>

I want to thank my mother, Catherine Coleman-Myers, for her love, devotion, and support. You have brought a depth of love, trust, and devotion to God that has navigated my life experiences. You taught me how to stand in the face of storms and profit from each one.

Kudos to my daughter, Catherine Nichole, and my granddaughter, Amile, for allowing me to dip my toes in deep unknown waters. The two of you have been my cheerleaders and champions. You understood my need to do and be more in this season of life.

Kiese Laymon, my wonderful nephew, you inspire me! I am so proud of the grace that rests on your life. Keep helping the world with your mind's genius and your pen's scripting.

To my sisters, Linda and Mary, thank you for the life lessons and friendship of sisterhood. You have each inspired and encouraged me.

I am so thankful for the love, commitment, and dedication of my TA&O Church family. It is a great honor to lead such wonderful, faithful men and women of God.

To all my sons and daughters in the gospel, keep being lights in the face of darkness. The greater works are bidding you to rise and step forward. You have what it takes to help change the world for the good.

To the powerful women in this anthology, thank you, thank you, thank you for believing in this God-ordained body of work.

Dr. Catherine Coleman

I would like to thank my mother, Carolyn Coleman, for her patience, love and encouragement. You have encouraged and pushed me to dream bigger and never quit on life.

To my precious daughter, Amiel, you inspire me. You are such a precious gift from God. I love and pray for your health, happiness, joy, prosperity, and peace.

To my namesake Granny, how do I say thank you? Your life is my inspiration. Your courage in the fire has built up my faith muscles. Thank you for being my granny and now my friend.

To my aunts, Linda and Mary, thank you for being, giving, and sharing in my growth and development. I love you.

To my cousin, Kiese Laymon, your drive, courage to love and forgive has brought light, love, and laughter to the family. So proud of you. You inspire me. Thank you for all that you do.

To my TA&O Family, Crowned in Royalty Family and the community at large, it has been a privilege serving, advocating and working with you. I love and appreciate each of you.

Dawn Dean

First and foremost, praises and thanks to a Mighty God. For He knew His plans were to prosper me, not harm.

I would not be who I am today if Willie Dean (grandfather) had not taught me how to write the alphabet and string words together to form a sentence. If my two mothers, Elizabeth Dean (grandmother) and Carolyn Dean (mother), had not given me the gift of life and love. If my aunts, Frances and Polly, and cousin, Jackie, had not been the very depiction of what a strong unstoppable black woman looked like. They all guide me from heaven now. Without their influence, I would not be who I have become.

Thank you, Dr. Carolyn Coleman, for your wisdom, believing in me, and allowing God to use you in the most magnificent ways.

Special thanks to my children and grandchildren for always supporting and loving me as I am.

Nitza M. Diaz

I would like to thank God for giving me courage to be bold to write stories that heal.

Abuela Minga, thank you for modeling boldness and courage! See you in Heaven!

Dad and Mom, thank you for always reminding me to be bold and courageous and to trust God with everything!

To my siblings, thank you for loving me!

Emmanuel, Matias and Victoria, thank you for your patience and forever love!

To my husband Edward, I love you! Your patience and love truly show God's intention for marriage!

Dr. Keisha Fleming

First, I would like to thank and give honor to my Heavenly Father, the author and finisher of my life. Thanks to my son, Dre, my siblings, family, and friends for their support and encouragement. To my Spiritual Father, Bishop-Prophet Antoine M. Jasmine, your divine wisdom has been the light through my darkest hours. Thank you for seeing greatness within me when I couldn't recognize it in myself. Special thanks to Bishop Carolyn Coleman for the encouraging words, challenging me, and giving me an opportunity to "grow" into this great journey that I have embarked upon. Lastly, to my parents, Felton and Barbara Edwards Fleming, who are absent from the body but present with the Lord, I hope that I have made you proud by continually fulfilling generational purpose. I love and miss you both beyond words. Thank you for "setting me apart" even when I didn't understand the reason.

Pamela Grant

I would like to thank God for His unconditional love and faithfulness towards me and this opportunity to become an author that I never dreamed possible. You allowed me to see more in myself than I could ever imagine.

To my family that was surprised I accomplished this journey, each of you, without knowing, inspired me to do something out of my norm. I love you and I give a special thanks to my grandson who purchased my first book.

To my friends and everyone who supported me by purchasing a book, I appreciate you. Blessings, love and prayers to each of you.

A special thank you to my greatest encouragers…The Trail Blazers.

Last, in loving memory of my mother and father for your love and giving me space to grow into the strong faithful woman you both encouraged me to be.

Patricia Jackson

I am deeply grateful to the many individuals who have contributed to the creation and completion of this book. Their support, guidance, and encouragement have been invaluable throughout this journey, and I am honored to express my heartfelt appreciation.

I would also like to express my deepest appreciation to my family and friends who have stood by me with unwavering support and encouragement. Your love,

understanding, and patience have been a constant source of motivation, and I am grateful beyond words for your presence in my life.

Parents – Claiborne and Lillie Mae Maten-Dailey; Husband – Pastor Russell Jackson; Children - D'Angela Patterson and Patrick Dailey; Bonus Children – Danielle Battiste, Gerrord Jackson, Hope J. Battiste, and Eric Jackson; Friend/Sisters – Dr. Shannon Johnson and Lady Beverly Honore'; Aunt – Mary J. Simon; and Special Cousin/Sister – Sandra Signater.

A special acknowledgment goes to Dr. Carolyn Coleman who worked tirelessly to bring this book to fruition. Your professionalism, attention to detail, and commitment to excellence have been truly remarkable. Thank you for believing in this project and for your unwavering support throughout the publishing process.

Lastly, I would like to thank the readers of this book. It is your curiosity, engagement, and support that make the publication of this work worthwhile. I hope that the ideas and insights presented within these pages resonate with you and contribute to your intellectual journey.

In conclusion, writing these letters has been a collaborative effort, and I am indebted to the numerous individuals who have played a part in its creation. Your contributions, whether big or small, have made a significant impact, and I am truly grateful for your support. Thank you all for being an integral part of this endeavor.

Dr. G. Landry

I would like to acknowledge my Lord and Savior for giving me the ability to accomplish all that I do. Without Him none of this would be. So, Thank You, Father.

Mei Mak

To God be the glory. I wanted to acknowledge and thank our Heavenly Father for all He has done for us, including this amazing anthology. I also thank my husband and children for their love and support whilst writing this book.

Lana M. McQuinn

I'd like to acknowledge my Lord and Savior Jesus Christ for giving me the opportunity to co-write this book with my fellow authors. I'd like to acknowledge first and foremost my children, my son, Michael, and wife, Jessica, and grandchildren, my daughter, Zsnita, and husband, Damian, and grandchildren. I thank you so much for being so supportive and encouraging me in everything that I do. I love you.

I would like to thank my Prelate, Bishop, Prophet, Pastor, Provoker, Spiritual Father Bishop Charles A. Ross for always encouraging me to move forward and stay in the will of God. Thank you.

I would like to acknowledge my Coach, Counselor, Dean, Dr. CC, Mama CC, Bishop Carolyn Coleman for all that you have done for me.

I would like to acknowledge my family, my mother, Eloise Lewis, my grandparents, my siblings, uncles and aunts. I thank you all for your love.

I'd like to acknowledge Evangelist Helen Hockett who helped me on my journey from the beginning. Apostle Andrew and Jacqueline Fulgham, thank you for all that you've taught me. Thank you, my First Lady JaQuanda Ross, for always encouraging me. Thank you, Bishop Marlon Baker, for always praying. Thank you, Pastor Bannister, for being the prayer warrior/intercessor. Thank you, Dr. Claudette Bryant-Claire, for always encouraging me. Thank you, Tina Sanders, my best friend. Thank you, Dr. Nicole Coleman for everything. I love you.

Elizabeth Miller

I would like to acknowledge my Lord and Savior, who is the head of my life, for loving me for just who I am. And to my daughters and grandchildren and family and friends, thank you for your love and support, for keeping me encouraged, for pushing me into my purpose, and for your continued gravity for more to come in my life.

Dr. Linda Roberson

Words cannot express my deepest love and gratitude to God. It is He who causes me to triumph in all things. Without Him, I am nothing. Because of His healing in my life, I am able to help others to heal. For this privilege, I am grateful.

I would like to thank my siblings, Rev. Dr. Valentine Sutton-Page and Johnnie Roberson, Jr., who have continually encouraged and supported me, even when they did not realize that they were doing so. I love and thank God for you.

To you, the individual reading this book, thank you for choosing it. It was destined for you to have. As God begins, continues and completes your healing, trust and know there is nothing that He cannot do. Allow Him to touch your deepest pain and bring the necessary healing that only He can give. He is the God who heals us.

Apostle Rose Ann Thomas

I thank God who is the head of my life for the courage, strength, and faith to believe that I could write and share my story.

To my grandsons, Justin and Xavier Hawkins, thanks for pushing and believing in me and my ministry. Truly you are my angels in the earth realm. I thank God for the gift of grandsons. I love you two for being my helpers and encouragers.

To my children, Angela, Nikki, Cedric, Kenney, and Laronda, I love you and daily speak blessings over your lives.

To my husband, Frederick, and all my grandchildren and siblings, I love you.

I applaud and thank God daily for my Church Family. Thank you for your dedication, love, and care. I love, value, and appreciate the Liberty Family Life Center and

New Envision Faith Tabernacle. I know that if it had not been for the Lord on my side, none of this could have happened.

I shout hallelujah for my teacher and encourager who inspired me through this writing journey, Dr. C. Coleman aka The Lady of Wisdom.

Thank you to Dr. Linda Roberson and all my supporters.

Penelope Tiam-Fook

I would like to give my thanks to Dr. Carolyn Coleman for the opportunity to include my letters of healing in this anthology. I was excited when I learned Dr. Coleman was working on an anthology, and joyful when she invited me to submit my letters to join her co-authors to inspire God's children to heal their hearts, mind, body, and soul. Dr. Coleman is one of the most committed prayer warriors I am fortunate to know, and she inspired me to keep on praying for others both in a small group and in private.

I am forever thankful to God for encouraging me and listening to my every prayer when my health took a turn for the worse over three years ago after being diagnosed with Lyme Disease. Lyme turned my world upside down, yet I am thankful that I listened to God's prompting to make time every day to believe in and embody the healing power of Jesus Christ to deliver me from the worst days of this disease.

My heart is filled with deep gratitude and appreciation for my family who experienced my journey towards restoration and all the in-betweens. I am especially thankful to my mom and stepfather (may his soul rest in peace) who always believed in me, and my daughter and her father who kept me motivated to reclaim my health to be a very present mom indeed. It's because of your support that I am thriving today.

Last yet certainly not least is a woman God placed in my life for a reason and hopefully a very long season, Dawn Dean, author and wellness writer. I cherish your friendship and your gentle yet committed nudges to share my writing with the world. May this be the first of many writings to be shared with the world, God willing!

Shalonda "Treasure" Williams-Lynard

I just want to say thank You, Oh Great I AM, for life, love and Shalom. Thank you, Dr. C.C., for the opportunity to give strength to another in this blessed world. Thank you, husband, Mr. Marco Lynard, for always supporting me. I'm forever grateful.